THE CHAIN

THE CHAIN

A Memoir & Reimagined Biography

Brandee Radford

Brandee Radford
The Chain

First Edition

Paperback ISBN 978-1-7781673-2-4
Hardcover ISBN 978-1-7781673-1-7
Ebook ISBN 978-1-7781673-0-0

Book Design | Petya Tsankova
Editor | Lori Bamber
Publishing Support | TSPA The Self Publishing Agency, Inc.

In memory of my father, Walter Pustey.
(1931 -2016)

In you, I saw a true writer.

The greatest source of learning is the experience of adventure.

Author Unknown

To quote the great Shonda Rhimes and the opening of *The Anna Delvey Story*:

"This whole story is completely true, except for all the parts that are totally made up."

For Kate's story, I relied first on many books and articles written about her life, the most important of which are listed on the reference page. But to bring her to life and fill in the gaps in her history, I've applied my experiences in Dawson City and my imagination.

For my own story, I've changed names, dates and a few details, sometimes to protect the privacy of others. In general, my intent is to provide "deniability"—the opportunity to say, "That wasn't me, I didn't do that, she's lying."

This is my story. I leave it to you to decide what's "true."

CONTENTS

CHAPTER ONE

Getting a whole new life wasn't as hard as I expected.

I'd left home at fifteen, sure that romance and adventure were waiting for me nearby, and I just had to go find them.

I found parties, some drugs, too much alcohol, and a patched-together life waitressing in small towns to pay the rent on sketchy apartments.

By the time I hit my mid-twenties, it was clear even to me that I'd headed down the wrong path and needed a new one. I talked to a social worker, and she helped me apply for a grant to cover the cost of a travel agent course. World travel was my dream, so it seemed like the perfect career.

I moved to the city.

At dawn one morning, I found myself rolling my extensive penny collection into small cardboard cylinders, sixteen of them, at my tiny kitchen table. It wasn't possible to enjoy my morning coffee without a cigarette, and I'd run out late the night before.

I pushed start on the coffee maker, grabbed my jacket, and headed down to the corner market at the end of my block.

Embarrassed, I handed over eight dollars' worth of copper pennies in a plastic bread bag. The clerk rolled her eyes.

Behind me, some guy laughed, and someone said, "Fuck, are you kidding?"

I pretended to ignore the remark, but I was mortified.

Then something shifted in me. It felt instant, but I've since come to understand that sudden changes almost always happen after things have been shifting underground for a while. That's the way it's been for me, at least.

I'd built a wee bit of self-esteem qualifying for the study grant and working hard on my course assignments, and now it felt dumb to spend money on something that caused cancer and made my hair smell bad. I thought about standing in the rain outside restaurants, my hair flattened to my face, freezing, just to get that fix, and the mental image made me furious.

I had dinner with friends at a Chinese diner that night, and after we ate, I felt around in my jacket pocket and pulled out a half-smoked cigarette that I'd saved for this moment. I held it up.

"After this, I quit!"

When the waitress came by, I surprised her by handing over all the lighters and matches I had collected in my rather large purse.

"Please throw all this into the garbage—I'm quitting!"

We celebrated together. I had made the decision to change my life for the better, and this was one more step in that direction.

Quitting gave me new energy to solve another problem: I was lonely. About a month after moving to the city, I decided it was time to date. I'd always fallen for the wrong type of guy, but this time, I was determined to change that pattern.

Back then there was no such thing as online dating, so I took out an ad in the newspaper.

Desperately seeking Romeo:
Romeo must be tall, dark and handsome; adventurous, silly, romantic and LOVE to travel.
Juliet is 5' 7," blonde with blue eyes. Spontaneous, funny, loyal and loves long walks, holding hands and big white snowflakes.

Yeah, I know. Not "must be kind"—just handsome, romantic and adventurous. What can I say?

It was the nineties, and my friends met their mates at bars or work like normal people. But I was on a new path that called for new methods.

"Blond and blue-eyed" seemed to do the trick from the men's side of things, and the replies started to come in. After a couple of false starts, I received a message from someone who seemed intriguing and gave him a call. We spent hours on the phone that first night, then every night after that for a few weeks.

Finally, we arranged our first date.

All I knew was that he would pick me up on the following Saturday morning and that I was to dress "really warm."

When Saturday came, I threw on all the layers I had and waddled out my door and into the elevator. He was waiting by the curb outside of my building in a silver and blue Dodge pickup.

I have to admit I was a little letdown. He did not have dark hair, and he wasn't as handsome as I'd hoped, two of the main requirements of my ad. But I am not the kind of person who would intentionally hurt someone's feelings, so I climbed clumsily into the truck and he pulled out from the curb.

Then I panicked. I was now in a vehicle with a stranger, driving off to who knows where. I was so naive back then—I hadn't even thought about the possible dangers until I was all the way in. Luckily for me, Dean was not a serial killer.

It was easy to talk to him as we drove, and we'd had so many telephone conversations that I felt comfortable.

"So, where are you taking me?" I asked. "I hope I'm dressed warmly enough!"

I was so bundled up that I could barely bend at the waist to sit. I must have looked at least twenty pounds heavier than the nicely curvy hundred and thirty pounds I was.

He gave me a cute sideways half-grin and said, "Can you ski?

"SKI?! No!!"

"Well, that's where I'm taking you. It's easy."

"Easy?! I don't even have any ski gear!"

I was worried.

"I brought you some. It's pretty much new—you can keep it if it fits." He laughed. "If you remove a layer or two, it just might be your size."

On the hill, he pulled a black hockey bag out of the back of the truck and brought out a purple two-piece ski outfit.

Cute! It was even my colour.

I slid out of the long johns I had on over my pants. As I pulled one of my many sweaters up and over my head, my hair caught in the buttons.

Dean came over and gently, patiently untangled it.

I stepped into the ski pants, tucked in my shirt, and zipped up the jacket.

"How do I look?" I asked, twirling to show him the full effect.

His eyes lit up. "It looks like it was made for you."

He brought out the boots and skis.

"They were my wife's," he said quietly.

He'd told me on the phone that he had been married, and that his wife had died of cancer earlier that year.

I felt a bit strange stepping into another woman's clothing, a woman who was no longer around to give me her permission, but it seemed insensitive to say anything.

Dean helped me put on the skis, the brilliant sun reflecting off the snow and warming us both.

I'd never thought of trying to ski before—it just hadn't come up. Now I didn't think there was even a slight chance I could move from the spot I was standing in, let alone get all the way up to the bunny hill. But slowly I began to push off and slide at the same time. I was skiing!

"How do we get to the top of the hill?" I asked, totally clueless.

"See that rope?" he said, pointing at the tow line off to the side. "You grab onto that with both hands, and it will pull you to the top."

"Okay, let's go!" I said, laughing, feeling more confident now that I'd stayed upright for almost a minute.

Dean stayed right behind me as we were pulled to the top, laughing kids ahead of and behind us. I pushed away from the rope and stood looking down the hill.

I was terrified. "Oh, god. I don't know if I can do this!"

"It's a very small hill," Dean said. "Just push off."

A child of about four skied gracefully by me, so I did, deciding I wouldn't give it another thought.

Dean was right. I didn't fall once on my first try.

After a few uneventful runs, I said, "I wish I could go faster."

He came up behind me and put his hands gently on my waist, leaning in. I could feel his breath on my neck, moving my hair. I felt a warm, unsettling sensation—one I'd really missed since my last relationship had ended a year before.

"Okay," he said. "No matter what happens, keep your skis

between my skis and keep them pointed downhill. Okay?"

"Okay," I replied.

We pushed off.

Oh my god! I wanted to do it again and again. So, we did.

Then, on what turned out to be our last run, something happened. Suddenly my skis were tangled with his and we both went down hard, tumbling almost to the bottom of the hill before finally grinding to a stop. At one point, Dean cried out in pain.

I jumped up and ran after the skis he'd lent me; they'd come off and were still skidding away.

When I turned back, Dean sat holding one knee.

"Are you okay?" I asked.

He was pale, his expression tense.

"I don't know. It feels like something popped out," he said.

I helped him up and he asked if I'd hurt myself. As I said that I hadn't, our eyes met and we started laughing at the same time. I think we were both imagining what we'd looked like, skis and limbs tangled together, as we fell first one way and then another all the way down the hill.

With him leaning heavily on my shoulder, we managed to make our way back to his truck. His leg was already swelling quite a bit, so we headed home.

As I got out of the truck in front of my apartment, he grabbed my arm and pulled me over for a kiss. I wasn't really expecting it, given all the drama, but we'd had fun.

"Thanks for a great date. Very original and noteworthy," I said as I jumped enthusiastically out of the truck.

We laughed together again and he smiled at me as I closed the door. He had a great smile.

He proceeded to lay a little rubber as he drove away.

I didn't hear from Dean for a few days. It was the first time someone I'd gone on a date with hadn't called me immediately afterward, and it stung a bit.

I waited one more day, then decided to call him. When he answered after a few rings, I told him I was worried about his knee and thought I should check up on him.

"Yep. I just walked in from my physiotherapist appointment—he says I'll need a few weeks of therapy on it."

Then he suggested that we try another date, given that the first one hadn't gone as planned.

I agreed, telling myself it was because I felt terrible about his knee.

My birthday was a few days later and I guess I'd mentioned it in one of our telephone conversations because there was a knock at my door just after I got home from school. I looked through the peephole and saw a clown. Um, what!? I opened the door a crack with the security chain on, and he said he had a delivery for me.

I was as shocked by the huge flower arrangement as I was by the full-volume rendition of "Happy Birthday!" the clown then belted out in my hallway, my neighbours peeking out to see what was going on.

There were so many flowers he almost couldn't get them through the doorway.

Dean! I ran to the telephone to thank him. It was such a romantic thing to do and made me feel spoiled. I had a weakness for grand gestures, and in the past, my boyfriend picking up a six-pack on his way home and offering me one was about as grand as it got.

I was beginning to look forward to our next date. A lot.

Two weeks later, we had our second date. Once again, I had no idea where we were going.

A few minutes before he was scheduled to arrive, I heard horns honking furiously in front of my building. I ran to look out the window.

My street was narrow, with vehicles parked on both sides. Dean was driving his truck—with a startlingly large boat behind it. There was no way to get by him, so vehicles were backed up in either direction and everyone was pounding on their horns, including him.

I grabbed my purse and jacket and raced down the three flights of stairs.

Throwing open the truck door, I said, "Are you crazy?!"

"Jump in," he said, laughing. "We're going out on the ocean."

The ocean was something else that was new to me. I was afraid of open water, and I tended to get motion sickness—I wasn't going to be booking any sailing trips on my own.

I didn't tell him that.

The boat was beautiful, a 24-foot Bay-liner. He had prepared everything, bringing a delicious picnic lunch of sandwiches and salads from a local deli. There was a thermos of steaming coffee to keep us warm.

We sped through the waves, and I loved it. It was a perfect day to be on the water, and the wind whipped our hair behind us, the bright sun in our eyes. I could feel my heart pounding, but it was excitement, not fear. I was surprised to realize I didn't feel sick at all.

Then Dean cranked the wheel sharply to the right just as we came to a sudden, dead stop, knocking us both almost off our seats. "Shit!"

What the hell?

"We're high-centred on a sandbar," he yelled.

I couldn't believe it—we were miles from land!

We couldn't call anyone, as cellphones didn't exist yet, but we'd signed in at the private launch and Dean's truck was in their lot. We were pretty sure someone would eventually miss us.

We ate our lunch, drank the last of the coffee, and talked and laughed about being in yet another predicament together.

Eventually we both got chilled and decided to go below, curling up with a blanket on the bed to keep warm. It was cozy, and I soon fell asleep with his arms around me.

I woke after a few hours to the sound of waves, almost as if we were at the beach.

Dean opened his eyes a second later, and we got up and climbed the stairs. We looked over the side together and laughed—the tide had gone out and we could see how big the sandbar was. Whoops! So that's why there was a depth finder.

We were soon hungry and thirsty, but we found things to do to keep us occupied, and early the next morning, the tide finally lifted us high enough that we could shove off.

We headed right back, and as we neared the launch, we could see search and rescue trucks and a coast guard boat.

Everyone stopped what they were doing as we came in, their faces lit up with huge smiles.

Dean might not have been as handsome as I'd hoped, but he came with a double helping of adventurous—and he was different than anyone I'd ever met.

It didn't take long before I realized I was in love.

He proposed on a Caribbean cruise nine months later, inviting me to pick out a diamond in a lovely little jewelry store in Saint Martin. We were married in a small ceremony at my parents' home almost exactly a year after our second date.

My new life had arrived.

I quit school and moved in with Dean—we would travel the world together. The following spring, I joined my new husband as we headed to the Yukon to start our new venture.

Gold mining!

CHAPTER TWO

In late April 1997, we left home and drove to a small town in the interior of BC, about five hours from our home on the coast, to pick up Maddy. One of my best friends, she was one of those people we all need in our lives, with just the right amount of crazy.

She'd agreed to join our mining team as the camp cook, taking a summer leave from her regular job. She had no experience as a cook, but I knew she was hard-working and reliable because we'd met at work. It felt like we laughed all the time when we were together.

After loading her things into the back of the truck, we hit the road again, talking non-stop.

Our next destination was the home of Dean's long-time best friend, Shawn. A luxury log home builder by trade, he'd decided it was time to try his hand at something different, too. A deteriorating knee, lower back problems and marital unhappiness all contributed to his decision, and he seemed thrilled to join us. Dean was counting on Shawn to learn to operate heavy equipment and ultimately become our right-hand man.

We watched him say his goodbyes to his family as Dean stuffed his duffle bags, boots and guns into the back of the truck. Shawn had also decided to bring Sam along, his enormous white and black St. Bernard cross. I was happy to have a dog with us, even though Sam was goofy-looking and huge and slobbered everywhere all the time.

Maddy was immediately smitten with Shawn. Within minutes of pulling out of his driveway, she entertained us all by wrapping herself around him like a sleepy toddler wraps herself around her mama. Arms draped around his shoulders, she snuggled her face into his neck, throwing one leg over his hips so he could barely move. Really, who wouldn't be attracted to Shawn? He was a six-foot-tall Tom Cruise doppelgänger, slender but muscular, with a megawatt smile and a wicked sense of humour.

A bit shocked by Maddy's brazen behaviour, he said nothing at all. Only the colour of his face changed as he moved his head to look past her at the road ahead.

We all laughed, and kept on laughing. The four of us got along famously.

We drove long into the night, stopping only to eat and switch drivers. From Shawn's house, Whitehorse was a thirty-two-ish-hour drive without breaks. We were on a tight schedule because Dean had arranged to meet up with the bush pilot who would fly us into camp by helicopter from Dawson City, another six hours past Whitehorse.

The drive was gruelling. The farther north we drove, the colder it was outside the truck. Blackened spruce trees leaned like children's pick-up sticks, a drunken forest. The permafrost was heaving, pushing upwards, knocking its trees off-kilter. The whole scene looked eerie to me.

The moment we stepped out of the truck, harsh winds chilled us to the bone, blowing as though intent on extinguishing us.

At home, late April meant an abundance of blooming cherry trees and tulips surrounded by green grass and giant trees unfurling their new leaves. Here, icy snow blanketed the roads and the fields on either side; the hills glistened white. It was a masterpiece in barren monochrome.

Just outside of Watson Lake, a village on the historic mile 635 of the Alaska Highway, we learned one of the North's lessons the hard way—we ran out of gas.

The small town is famous for its sign-post forest. People from all over the world have nailed up handmade or stolen signs from their hometowns—the last time I was there, there were more than seventy-eight thousand. But all we cared about at that moment was its gas station, the first and last for many, many miles.

It was still dark when we sputtered to a stop. We sat for a while in the freezing truck, huddling together for warmth, until Dean remembered that he had filled both of our ATVs with gas before loading them. They were deep in the back of the cargo trailer we were hauling behind us.

As quickly as we could, we unloaded suitcases, bedding, dog food, groceries, first aid supplies and equipment until we finally uncovered one. Dean and Shawn managed to syphon enough gas to get us into town, but only after Shawn swallowed a bit, gagging until he threw up. I felt awful for him—just the smell made me feel sick too.

We made it to the gas station and waited in the parking lot. When the attendant finally flipped on the open sign, Maddy and I raced inside to find the bathroom and warm up.

We eventually made it to Whitehorse, a quaint, bustling city named after the rapids on the Yukon River, said to look like the manes of charging white horses. We arrived late in the afternoon, but with sunset at around ten at night, we had plenty of time to get the rest of our supplies.

The North in late spring and summer is a surreal experience. It felt magical to get lost in time as the days stretched to midnight. I'd often work into the wee hours of the morning there, startled when I finally ran out of energy and checked the time. From June until September, we enjoyed almost twenty-four hours of daylight.

That day in Whitehorse, we spent four or five hours trudging from machine parts stores to hardware stores to grocery stores, gathering everything we'd need for our first few weeks in camp.

When our chores were complete, we drove to the home of one of Maddy's friends, the four of us descending on her cozy house on the outskirts of the city. She kindly let us all shower and clean ourselves up. It felt inexpressibly wonderful to stand under hot water after so many hours stuffed into a truck cab meant to seat three. Thirty-two hours of rough, unending highway, packed like a can of sardines? It's a true test of friendship. It was impossible to get comfortable, our asses and backs hurt, we couldn't sleep, and we ate junk food to kill the boredom until we felt sick.

The mere thought of even one more hour in that damn truck was torture, but we ate a quick dinner, drank yet more coffee and set off again, this time for Dawson City. We'd heard this stretch of road would be some of the worst because the frost creates huge potholes—brutal!

The trees in the Yukon grow to only a quarter of their potential size, the effect almost as if forest fires had recently passed through. But there was so much wildlife, too.

One of the sweetest things I have ever laid eyes on was a mama bear with her tiny cubs playing right in the middle of the road ahead of us. The cubs didn't seem to have a care in the world as they rolled across the pavement in a family wrestling match.

We stopped the truck and stepped out quietly to watch them.

Snowflakes fell gently on us all, melting almost instantly on their thick brown jackets. Steam rose from their fur, making for a striking photo to add to my growing album. Except for their occasional little squeaks, everything around us but the wind was completely silent. We were in a new world, one I'd never imagined.

We finally arrived in Dawson City, which, to clear things up right away, is not a city. It lovingly refers to itself as the "wildest little town in the Yukon, home to the colourful 5%!" Built on permafrost, almost every building sits on stilts, and the population tops out at around nineteen hundred.

It wasn't always small. Dawson is the heart of the Klondike Valley and its population reached forty thousand by the end of the gold rush in the late 1890s. Today, it's made up of small, dilapidated buildings painted in a multitude of vibrant colours, including sunny yellow, royal purple, every shade of green and flamingo pink.

I fell instantly in love with its quirkiness.

It was quiet when we arrived, its extraordinarily wide roads a mix of dirt and gravel. A sign perched high on a metal pole identified Front Street, along which we saw restaurants, coffee shops and jewelry and clothing stores.

We searched the dusty street for an open restaurant before realizing we were early. The four of us once again snuggled into the truck together for a few winks of restless sleep.

As soon as the first restaurant flicked on its lights, we hustled our freezing butts into its cozy interior.

Piles of crispy bacon and eggs, toasted homemade marble rye bread dripping with butter—what a glorious way to start the day! All four of us were weary but excited about the day ahead too. The skies were as blue as robins' eggs and the wind that had been blowing for days was suddenly still. It was balmy, the temperature just below freezing. In the sun, it was almost warm enough to take off my jacket.

After breakfast, Maddy and I were sent to pick up supplies for the next leg of our trip.

Maddy, Dean and I were heading out to our mining site, an hour-long flight away.

"Pick up food for three big lunches," he said. "Oh, and something to drink. It will be a long day."

No problem.

We all met back at the truck a few hours later, in a rush because we were now late to meet the pilot at the helicopter pad about ten minutes from downtown. Shawn drove as fast as the truck would go, and we all hoped the pilot was having a good day.

I couldn't contain my delight when I saw the helicopter. It was a two-tone blue beauty, "Fireweed" written across the door in neon pink.

It was my first helicopter trip, and I was over-the-top excited and a bit scared.

I had been terrified of flying but my fears had all been pushed underground since meeting Dean. I felt like I was safe with him, and I was having the greatest time of my life.

We brought along three lunches, a large thermos of coffee, water, pop, warm jackets, boots and gloves. A backpack with an extra change of clothes for each of us in case we got wet. A Sony Walkman, my little black case filled with favourite CDs, and a couple of books I had picked up in Whitehorse.

Dean also brought his gun, his toolbox and a few cans of ether, explaining that it would help get the bulldozer started if it was too cold. It had sat idle for a long time.

We were to return by plane later that day, and Shawn would pick us up at the airport. In the meantime, he would arrange for our final flight into camp with our supplies the next day.

After loading our things into the helicopter, the three of us found our seats.

The pilot walked around to my side and leaned through the sliding door to hand us each a headset. He showed Maddy and me (the two giggling fools in the backseat) how to control the volume, explaining that everyone on board would hear us if we talked into the mouthpiece, but that only one person could be heard at a time.

He checked everyone's seatbelts, giving each one a solid yank to make sure they were tight. Pulling the heavy sliding door beside me closed, he locked it firmly into place.

He strapped himself into his seat and did an audio check, reminding us where to find the vomit bags. I'd often been motion sick in cars, so I paid careful attention.

The massive blades began to turn slowly. Through my window, I saw Shawn leaning against our truck and gave him a big smile and wave.

The blades were soon spinning at full speed, blowing the snow and dirt wildly around the hangar.

The pilot turned and looked back at Maddy and me, giving us the thumbs-up signal. We both smiled enthusiastically, mimicking his gesture.

It felt so strange, lifting off in a helicopter. It's different than in a plane because it's not gradual. It's more like the bottom falls out and you are suddenly in the air, a feeling I soon craved.

Through my small window, I could see Shawn holding onto his baseball cap with both hands as snow, ice and dirt swirled around him like a small tornado.

Dean looked back at me and laughed out loud at how excited I was.

We were soon over the nearby airstrip, banking slowly to the right and then flying due north.

For the first time, I saw the enormity of the destruction created by the mining that stripped the local creeks of dirt, rocks and trees. I was astonished—and saddened—by how awful it all looked as we flew over one mine site after another. The gold camps were all silent at this time of the year, waiting for the miners to arrive. Like us, they were coming from all parts of the world to open their camps and prepare for the short working season ahead.

I asked Dean and the pilot a hundred questions, I'm sure.

The mining camps finally faded away, and we flew over a vast wilderness of trees, tundra, mountains, hills, rivers and creeks. I was quiet, thinking how lucky I was to be there.

Growing up, my family's biggest adventures were long drives in the family sedan to visit relatives or much-anticipated camping trips. I had only been on an airplane once before meeting Dean, a trip with friends to Mexico when I was about twenty.

I knew early on that I wanted to travel and do exciting things. I was a rebel, constantly in trouble in my teenage years, often running away from home. I had a deep longing to break away from small-town life and explore everything the world had to offer. In my heart, I somehow knew that I would, and I just couldn't wait to start.

My mother often asked questions like, "Where on earth did you come from?" and "Who do you think you are? Because you certainly don't act like my child."

The truth is that I didn't feel like her child either. I didn't feel like I belonged in my family for many years.

Now I was lost in wonder at the scene below me, just breathing it all in. On the inside, I was smiling a bigger smile than I'd ever smiled before.

I was jolted out of that sweet moment by reverberating crunching noises. It sounded like a rhino eating whole bunches of celery. I looked around and realized that Maddy was stuffing potato chips into her mouth, lost in her own moment and totally oblivious to the fact that she was deafening everyone on board.

I leaned over and whacked her on the arm, motioning that her crunching was being heard through the headsets. We broke into fits of laughter again and had to take our headsets off to avoid further auditory damage to Dean and the pilot.

After about an hour, we saw the Yukon River below us as we banked to the right, winding its way through the valley like a snake. A few minutes later, the pilot pointed out a flat spot where we could land, but Dean asked him to fly to the top of a mountain first.

Our main job that day was moving a large bulldozer from our drop-off point at the bottom of the mountain to the camp airstrip near the top.

Dean wanted to get a quick look at the road to see what we were in for.

The mountain was barren, a narrow dirt road etched into its sides and winding around the base. It had been extensively drilled and tested years earlier by a large hard-rock mining company. They didn't find enough copper, silver or gold and abandoned the project. The camp had sat, boarded up, for years; the CEO was more than happy to rent it to us for the summer.

At the top, we flew over seven or eight modular trailers, spaced out just enough to park vehicles and ATVs between.

As the pilot circled, Dean looked concerned. "This doesn't

look good," he said. "I wasn't expecting to see so much white stuff. It might take longer than I'd thought to move the dozer. Let's head back and get at it."

We touched down at the bottom of the valley, where the Canadian and Britannia creeks intersected. The pilot turned off the engine and, when it was safe, jumped out and opened the doors for us. When the blades finally came to a complete stop, we began unloading.

We were even further north now and had daylight until around eleven, giving us what felt like plenty of time.

We waved our goodbyes to the pilot as he fastened his seatbelt and restarted the engine. The blades began to spin, and the wind picked up speed. I held my hair back and closed my eyes, the dirt whipping around my face.

As the sound of the rotating blades faded into the morning light, I was struck by the quiet. Gradually I heard sparrows chirping and the rush of the nearby creeks.

It was a beautiful, warm morning, and I wore a light blue windbreaker, runners and sunglasses. I was so naive about absolutely everything at that time in my life—the implications of being dropped off in the middle of the wilderness without any means of communication didn't sink in at all.

Sudden weather changes occur like clockwork in the Yukon, but I was just following Dean's lead and had zero idea there was no plan B if we needed help.

As the years went on, I learned to be more careful. More careful, and more afraid.

I looked around and saw the huge yellow and black bulldozer, large block letters spelling out the universally recognized

Caterpillar logo. It sat among a few large red metal drums Dean said were full of diesel. Boxes and parts were strewn about, and a pile of black plastic motor oil buckets sat nearby.

Off to one side was another giant machine with a large digging bucket that I would later learn was an excavator.

The excavator was intimidating but nothing like the bulldozer. It was so massive I was terrified to even get close.

After Dean examined the boxes and buckets, he pulled himself up onto the tracks of the Cat and then onto a flat metal platform by the door. He peered into the cab through the dust-covered window.

"Come on up," he called out to me, grinning.

I pretended like it was nothing for me to do that. I was petrified.

"Just grab hold of whatever you can to pull yourself up," he yelled down.

I stood at the bottom looking up. The cold, slippery metal tracks went up well over my head.

Dean pointed out spots that were built as holds. Taking slow, deep breaths to help control my shaking hands and legs, I made my way up and stood next to him. I was scared to stand completely upright and even more afraid to look down.

I had always been afraid of heights, and now I was a long way up.

I tried to pretend everything was cool. Cool, cool.

Dean pulled the cab door open, settled into the operator's seat and motioned me inside. There was only one seat, so I sat on his knee, which would become my usual spot as he taught me how to run the Cat and the excavator. I spent many hours on his lap or squished in beside him, watching everything he did, preparing to run these massive machines myself. At the time, it seemed insane that I would even think about it, but I knew what I'd signed up for. Sort of.

Dean dug around in his pockets for the keys and then tried to start the engine. It wouldn't turn over. He tried a few more times before yelling down to Maddy to bring the cans of ether. He met her on the ground, and, giving the can a good shake, crawled onto the engine compartment.

To me, he yelled, "Turn the key. I'll spray ether into the engine intake to get it to crank."

I panicked. "What if it starts to move? What if I can't turn it off?"

He laughed. "It won't move. Don't worry."

I cautiously turned the key, and the engine coughed and sputtered as it tried to start. Dean began to spray the ether in small, short bursts every few seconds.

"Keep the key turned over," he said. "Whatever you do, don't turn it off."

Finally, the engine let out a cough and then a growl. Then it began to roar, coming to life.

I let go of the key and sat still on my seat, scared to move an inch. I didn't want to accidentally touch any of the controls near me.

Gathering everything we had brought with us from Dawson, we helped Maddy up onto the cab.

We were ready to head for the top of Casino Mountain, which we'd been told would take about four or five hours, depending on the road conditions.

There was only one seat, meant for the operator, and there were three of us, plus our backpacks, lunches, boots and warm jackets.

Maddy and I used all the padding we had—paper towels, toilet paper and our jackets—to try to make a tolerable place to sit. She positioned herself first, on the small, hard metal ledge that housed the controls for the blade in front and the ripper tooth on the back. She pulled her knees up to her chest and leaned on the glass window behind her. I sat in a similar position in front of her, her bony knees my backrest.

We were as comfortable as we could get, with no idea at all how rough our trip was going to be.

Dean shoved everything else we'd brought behind his seat and adjusted his comfy chair. Closing the cab door, he looked at the two of us, his eyes bright.

Smiling his trademark heart-melting grin, he grabbed my hand.

"Ready?"

CHAPTER THREE

The first hour on the narrow dirt road was all laughs and questions for Dean. I was particularly interested in the operation of the bulldozer, and he was more than willing to let me help.

He showed me how to control its direction by slowly pushing on the levers in front of where I was sitting. If I pushed the right lever forward, the machine turned to the left. If I moved the left lever forward, the machine turned to the right. Pushing both at the same time moved the Cat straight forward. If I wanted to go backwards, I pulled the levers back. I loved my new powers and felt slightly less intimidated.

After a few hours, we stopped to stretch and eat. The air smelled so fresh, and it was incredibly peaceful. I felt a bit like Cinderella in the Disney movie, with birds singing to me from every tree. I was almost overwhelmed by a sense of freedom and excitement about what was to come.

I had never been happier.

Maddy proudly produced our lunches, and we ate our slightly squished sandwiches leaning against the giant tracks. Dean poured us each a cup of still-steaming coffee from the thermos.

Then we were ready to set out again.

Maddy and I fluffed up the padding on our metal ledge,

trying desperately to make it a bit more comfortable. Our compacted bodies automatically fought for one more inch of space. It was incredibly awkward and painful, yet we both managed to fall asleep, not waking for some ninety minutes.

I opened my eyes as we crested the mountain, stunned to realize I had slept in such physical misery. I tried to sit upright to stretch my aching back, waking Maddy. I looked down to see I'd slobbered all over my jacket and wiped the side of my cheek with my hand, hoping no one else had noticed.

When he saw we were awake, Dean said we were incredibly lucky we'd fallen asleep. The road was so narrow in a few spots, he'd been afraid we would go over the side and roll back down the bank. He vividly described how the left track of the bulldozer had hung over the edge, threatening to topple the whole machine over the bank as the dirt crumbled away beneath it.

Somehow, I minimized what he'd just told us—surely it couldn't have been that bad, or he would have stopped, right? Moving on ...

The fog started to clear from my head as I saw how much snow there was on the ground. It was much colder up here, and we could hear the wind blowing hard outside the cab.

Straight ahead was a large hill, completely barren, with strange roads winding around it like a corkscrew. This was where the mining company had drilled years before.

We finally made it to the airstrip where our pilot would be landing in a few hours. We had to hurry and clear the snow so he could land safely.

Dean told Maddy and me to jump out and go find the old camp that would be our home for the summer.

I took off my running shoes and slipped on the winter boots I'd brought, pulling on my warm jacket, gloves and toque.

When I jumped down, I sunk almost to the top of my furry boots. The depth of the snowbanks was deceiving from our high, toasty cab.

We left Dean to clear the snow from the airstrip.

"Don't get lost!" he yelled, pointing in the general direction of the camp. "It's about twenty minutes down the road."

Maddy and I thought it would be faster if we just went over and down the bank, so we started down, knee-deep in snow drifts, our boots filling with each step we took.

We laughed hard at the predicament we had put ourselves in. By the time we reached the camp, our feet were soaked and we were both freezing and exhausted from dragging ourselves through the snow and brush. So much for shortcuts.

The camp was a conglomeration of rugged-looking, forest green and white modular trailers. The largest, shaped like a letter T, was a commercial kitchen with a dining area, and showers and toilets at the opposite end. Sleeping quarters for the cooks and janitorial crew were attached, ten tiny bedrooms.

Between the two of us, we managed to pull off the sheet of plywood nailed over the entrance door. It looked as though something had used its claws to rip some of the weathered wood off, and the nails were rusty from years of brutal winters and hot summers. There was no protection from the elements as the camp sat in an open dirt clearing.

The other trailers haphazardly scattered around the camp were dormitory-style housing for the crew and management. Each bedroom had a single metal bed frame with an old mattress, a small table, and a tiny closet in each corner. Some had tattered curtains or a sheet nailed across the window.

We worked our way through each room, looking through drawers and opening closets.

In the dining area, there were two long wooden tables with metal folding legs, a bunch of uncomfortable-looking wooden chairs stacked in the corner, and a rusty cast-iron wood stove in the centre. The stove pipe had fallen from the wall where it vented, leaving a hole large enough for squirrels and other critters to make their way inside. A few of the white fluorescent lights had detached from the ceiling and were hanging haphazardly or had dropped to the floor. Off to one side was a small sitting area with a couple of battered sofas and an old TV and VCR.

The kitchen was quite large, with rows of wooden shelves for supplies, an eight-burner propane cooktop, two large ovens, a huge flat-top griddle, three stainless steel sinks and loads of counter space. A table sat by a big window looking out over the valley and the view was breathtaking, miles and miles of mountain wilderness.

We continued to explore until Dean came in and said he was concerned about the weather. The clouds were low and dense, and he was expecting the airplane in the next half hour. Just as we were talking about it, we heard a faint engine sound in the distance. The three of us ran outside and up the road towards the airstrip.

My heart sank as I looked up, the clouds thick, black and so low to the ground it was almost like fog.

We could hear the engine's whir getting louder. Soon it was right above us, and we listened as it circled the airstrip two or three times. Then it turned back the way it had come.

The sound began to fade.

"Is he looking for another place to land?" I asked.

"Nope. We're here for the night," Dean said.

"Are you kidding?" Maddy and I blurted at the same time.

"I'm positive he'll be back first thing in the morning," he said.

I don't know why I hadn't considered the possibility of being stuck out here for the night, but it was a shock.

"We don't have any food or water. No one can contact us!" I felt a wave of panic swamping me.

As always, Dean seemed relaxed.

"Shawn and the pilot know where we are. They will be back as soon as the weather improves, probably tomorrow morning. Storms blow in without warning here—they usually last a day and then clear out."

I trusted him, and didn't worry too much after that.

I was in love.

We were having a great adventure.

Dean would keep us safe.

The summer before Dean and I met, he had spent a few months learning everything he could about mining. He had been a home builder in Vancouver and had done well for himself, but after his first wife passed away, he decided he wanted to change occupations. He'd told me soon after we met that the summer he spent mining was one of the best times in his life.

He'd had a strong desire to go prospecting even as a young man, so when an old friend offered him a job outside of Dawson City, he jumped at the chance. His friend taught him everything he knew about the placer mining industry.

By the time that summer was over, Dean definitely had "gold fever." Now I had it too.

He was full of stories about how we were going to get filthy stinking rich mining for gold. He had a way of making everyone around him believe that, if anyone could do it, it was him.

People believed in him. He was highly intelligent; I thought he was the smartest person I'd ever met. I'd watched him write down the answer to a complicated math question before the banker we were meeting with had a chance to pull out his calculator.

I had seen him in action many times at the meetings we had in preparation for our mining adventure. Dean included me in them all, and I listened raptly as he sold his ideas of fame and fortune to financial institutions, personal bankers and heavy equipment loan specialists.

He had the magic. He brought along a relish jar full of gold and photographs of mining sites, equipment and sluice plants. By the time he was done, the men he was speaking to were literally sitting on the edge of their seats, ready to quit their high-paying jobs and go mining with us.

That was just who he was—he could talk a monk into leaving the monastery to hunt for gold. It was an amazing thing to watch. Partly because of this, I trusted him more than I had ever trusted anyone. I trusted him completely.

We walked back down the hill to see what we could find to keep warm and prepare for the night ahead. I found a few tattered, smelly blankets in some of the trailer closets, and we dragged a couple of mattresses close to the wood stove. Dean worked on the stove pipe, reattaching it to the wall so the smoke would have a place to escape.

I asked Maddy what time it was and was shocked to learn it was almost eleven. We still had daylight!

Dean managed to get the stove fixed, and Maddy and I headed back outside to search for wood. We gathered sticks and dead branches and carried them back into the frigid trailer, and Dean found a small wood pile under cover near the back door that was fairly dry.

We were so happy sitting around that little stove, rubbing our hands together to warm them, our breath visible as we talked. But it wasn't long before we realized the space that we were trying to heat was much too large for one small stove.

Dean found another solution. Telling us to pick a bedroom, he pulled two of the beds together and put mattresses down on the metal frames. He set up a half-full propane bottle with a circular device attached to the top that he had found in one of the rooms. Soon he had it glowing red as heat poured off it. He set it to the lowest temperature, just enough to keep the frost out of the room. The three of us shared the few thin blankets we had, and snuggled together to keep warm.

Our laughter rang out in the empty hallways and through the abandoned camp, and we fell asleep fast.

I awoke to bright light seeping through the small window and its threadbare curtain. I sat up quickly, realizing that Dean was no longer in bed. Reaching over, I messed Maddy's hair. "Rise and shine, sleepyhead!"

I crawled over her and out of bed to look out the window. The clouds looked just as dense as they had the day before. My heart sank. Fuck!

"It doesn't look good," I said, as Maddy sat up in bed. "I don't know how the plane will land today if this doesn't get better."

The cold hit me hard as I opened the bedroom door. I found Dean in front of the stove, stuffing branches and small pieces of wood inside. He lit it and closed the creaky door. Soon the room began to warm slightly.

I asked what he thought the chances were of the airplane

getting in that day. He was quiet as he scanned the sky through the window.

"From what I can see now, it's highly unlikely. Unless the weather clears up."

We didn't have to worry about water, as there was tons of snow to melt and boil. The kitchen was full of pots and pans, so Maddy and I spent most of the day gathering and melting icy chunks we hauled in from the banks.

There was a weathered outhouse perched on the edge of the mountainside by the main camp trailer. It didn't have a door, but it did have the most beautiful view I'd ever seen: miles and miles of snow-capped peaks and wilderness. Despite the cold, I took my time on the padded toilet seat, marvelling at the spectacular nature before me.

We were starving and did a thorough search of the kitchen. The cupboards produced a few different flavours of Jell-O, a couple cans of fruit cocktail, a few cans of corn, and some cream of mushroom soup.

The best before dates were long past, but we were so hungry that Dean convinced us it would "probably be fine."

We managed to open some cans using a jackknife and ate soup and canned corn. We mixed the packages of Jell-O with fruit cocktail and melted snow to eat later. We also found a small jar of instant coffee and powdered coffee whitener.

Dean's confidence had eased my worries, and honestly, I was having more fun than I'd ever had. (Food poisoning hundreds of miles from the nearest hospital and no way to get there?! Pah!)

The next morning was stormy. Dean said that the "cloud ceiling" was still low, a measure he told me that pilots used when deciding whether or not to fly.

We were all so hungry and there was nothing left to eat, so we decided to go for a walk around camp and check out each of the crew quarters to take our minds off our stomachs.

On our way, I noticed large (huge!) bear tracks and yelled at Dean to come take a look.

"Yep, looks like they are out of hibernation. You two be careful—always pay attention to your surroundings. These look like grizzly from the length of the claws."

After snooping around for a bit, Maddy and I heard an engine start up. We looked outside to see Dean working on an old suburban-style vehicle. It was grey with lots of windows, MEDIC written on the side in red and white. Underneath was a red cross.

As he revved the engine, he yelled, "Well, we have a running vehicle."

He had found the keys in the ashtray and filled it with gasoline from a large barrel nearby. We all jumped in and drove up to the airstrip to make sure it was still clear.

Dean thought we should walk the strip and look for any big rocks that might cause the plane any trouble, so we did that for about an hour, throwing them off to the side.

We were walking back towards the suburban when I heard something and stopped.

"Yes! Yes!" I yelled, jumping up and down.

Maddy was screaming too, and Dean ran down the runway to move the suburban off to the side.

A large white dual-propeller plane burst through the clouds. It circled above us, its wings tilting sharply towards the ground as its engines slowed.

"Do you think he's going to land?" I yelled out to Dean.

"I think he's going to try!"

We were so happy! Maddy and I hugged and laughed.

"I hope Shawn brought food!" she said.

"And the satellite phone!" Dean added.

In the distance, the airplane dropped lower as it lined up with the runway. Its wings swayed from side to side, the high winds forcing it right and then left.

It wasn't an easy place to land a plane, the strip rocky and uneven, with a steep upward incline. Pilots did not like the Casino Mountain airstrip, I found out later, and it was the site of more than one crash.

I found myself praying for a safe landing.

Suddenly it slammed down, mud and snow exploding into the air.

It crested the hill slowly, gradually coming to a stop a few hundred feet from where the three of us stood.

The pilot waved and took his headset off. The white exterior was now muddy brown, and its nine tiny windows dripped with moisture.

This aircraft was lovingly referred to as "the Short," a nineteen-seat twin turbo used for short-haul freight and skydiving. This one was used mainly for hauling supplies and people in and out of remote mining camps.

Its large ramp creaked open and the pilot lowered it to the rough ground below.

Maddy and I ran around to the back just in time to see Shawn walk down the ramp, a huge grin on his face and a large watermelon in his arms.

Maddy bolted up the ramp and jumped on him. Her arms wrapped around him, she kissed his cheeks over and over before grabbing the watermelon and holding it above her head.

"My watermelon made it! In one piece!"

We all burst out laughing and then found we couldn't stop, dizzy with happiness, hunger and relief.

Maddy had lovingly tended to the watermelon all the way from her home. She announced when we first picked her up that, when the time was right, it was going to be the best watermelon we ever tasted. Now she kissed it and proudly handed it back to Dean, who produced his Swiss Army knife and carved it up on the backseat of the suburban. We one hundred percent agreed that it was the best damn watermelon we'd ever had!

Joyful didn't begin to describe us at that moment, the four amigos reunited after the storm. We talked over each other, Shawn asking lots of questions, Maddy and I telling him about the huge bear tracks and how we had lived off Jell-O and five-year-old cream of mushroom soup.

Dean was laughing and talking to the pilot. He looked over at me with that glimmer in his eye, the usual mischievous grin on his face.

We gleefully unloaded suitcases, water, the satellite phone, machine parts, and boxes of food. After filling the suburban to capacity, Maddy and I drove back down to camp to unload.

The guys stayed at the airstrip, rolling barrels of diesel and gasoline down the ramp and off to the side of the runway. Then they drove our shiny new ATVs out onto the road one by one, ready to explore. I looked forward to learning how to drive them.

The next few weeks were spent working around camp. Our priorities were to get the water running and rebuild the generator so we would have electricity. Maddy and I worked on cleaning all the bedrooms, and getting rid of the garbage that had been left to rot. It took us a week to get water, electricity and reliable heat. The day we turned on the lights was a celebration.

I was beginning to appreciate many things I had taken for granted, like electricity, running water and flushing toilets.

That first summer, the outhouse was our only option. I didn't like the smell much, or having to go outside late at night on my own in bear country. During the days, though, I often sat longer than I had to, just admiring the spectacular view. And when we returned to town, I appreciated flushing toilets so much more.

The days got even longer, and the weather warmer. After a big breakfast, Shawn and Dean drove the ATVs back down the mountain to put in a long day on our mining claims, preparing the ground so we could begin sluicing and catching gold.

Maddy and I baked, cleaned and cooked. I loved trying new recipes and made bread every day. In that clear, clean air, the smell of bread fresh from the oven was unforgettable. We read cookbooks and magazines until we were bored, then spent the rest of the day cleaning, chopping firewood, writing letters and exploring the mountain close to camp.

We had a satellite phone that might have been mistaken for a briefcase until you tried to lift it. It was about fifty pounds, with a satellite receiver built in. The receiver had to face a window, as close as you could get, so it could link to the satellite in space. Sometimes the reception was poor. Other times, especially on cloudy days, there was no reception at all. We could not count on the telephone.

I looked forward to the times I could call my family to tell them all about our great adventures. At that time, though, satellite phones were still a new technology, and we were charged $1.99 per minute. It added up fast. One month we had a shocking phone bill—over five thousand dollars! I started writing letters and sending them out with the pilots whenever we had supplies flown in, saving the telephone calls for parts and grocery orders.

We depended on our pilots for so much: picking up our groceries, equipment parts and supplies, and quite often transporting family and friends. They went to the banks for us, delivered gold to the local refinery, brought in staff, and mailed our parcels and letters.

Dean would sometimes have them pick up flowers or gifts for me, surprising me with something special. He was romantic and thoughtful that way.

I quickly felt trapped in the camp, and convinced Maddy that she would be fine on her own during the day. I wanted to see what was going on at the mine, and was keen to learn to use all the equipment. I wanted to mine for gold!

I had never understood why girls were always the ones in the kitchen and doing household chores. I wanted to learn, see and do. Luckily, Dean was the kind of man who wanted me to learn and be with him all the time, and it made him happy that I wanted that too.

I felt bad leaving Maddy on her own that first day, but adventure and gold were calling my name! We sped off on the ATVs, leaving a trail of dust behind us. I clung to Dean, my arms wrapped as tightly as they would go around him, the wind blowing hard in my face. I squinted, trying to see the road ahead through the tears that rolled down my cheeks.

I'm sure you could hear my laughter all through the valley as we raced Shawn down the twisted dirt roads.

CHAPTER FOUR

As we rounded the last corner, I realized we were back where the helicopter had dropped us off weeks earlier.

It all looked different now. The trees were greener and wildflowers had popped up everywhere. Fireweed grew tall on the roadsides and throughout the valley, its lilac and rose shades melding to create an ombre, spike-shaped flower. It spread as far as I could see. My love affair with fireweed began that day, and soon I was collecting it to make jelly, vinegars and soap. It was the focal point of countless wildflower bouquets I created for our tables during our years in the North.

Ahead of us was Britannia Creek, one of two creeks we would cross daily to reach our claims. That day, it was running fast and furious, rising higher by the minute. We sat and plotted how to safely get to the other side. It had doubled in size just since Dean and Shawn had crossed it late the night before on their way back to camp.

Winter had dumped a tremendous load of heavy snow on the mountains that rose above us. As the temperature climbed, the creeks and rivers became swollen with melt water. Gentle streams became treacherous, creating havoc for us.

We drove ahead cautiously, the water rising quickly over the running boards of the four-wheeler. I lifted my feet, stretching my legs straight out in front of me so the water could not fill my rubber boots. I held our paper bag lunches and backpacks over my head, my other arm wrapped tightly around Dean so I wouldn't tumble off.

He decided it was safe to go ahead and we roared through. The icy water sprayed high into the air, soaking us as it fell. We burst out laughing, both of us completely drenched!

The ATV clawed its way up the bank on the other side, its wheels throwing rocks and dirt back into the water. I hung on with all my might, worried I would fall off. We reached the top and stopped to look back just in time to see Shawn barrel through the creek as fast as he could. He, too, was now soaking wet.

Mud and water poured down our faces and off our clothes. We continued on, stopping for a few minutes to warm up each time we rode into a sunny spot.

It wasn't long before we came to the small clearing where the bulldozer and excavator sat among downed trees and uprooted stumps.

Dean and Shawn had been using the heavy machines to clear, pushing trees off the main valley as far as they would go. Sometimes thirty feet of trees, dirt and gravel had to be moved to reach the bedrock we needed to mine.

My first response was one of sadness. I was shocked to learn that trees that had taken decades to grow here would just be buried among the rocks, moss, dirt and gravel. Dean explained that it would cost more than the lumber was worth to drag the logs to the Yukon River and load them onto a barge. It just wasn't feasible.

It never stopped bothering me. I flew into Dawson City regularly, and from that high vantage point, I saw disregard for forests on a massive scale. Placer mining in the Yukon was big business; no one would dare try to stop it. "Mining is the backbone of the economy!" was the general response.

As is tourism—ironic.

Dean jumped off the four-wheeler and onto the bulldozer. The engine spurted, choked and coughed, and the black smoke poured out of the long metal stack perched on the hood. The thick smoke slowly mellowed to a light grey, and the Cat began to purr as it warmed up.

I climbed into the cab and squeezed myself onto the ledge beside the operator's seat, my spot for many hours that first year. I watched Dean's every move and asked a million questions. I learned as much as I could. Like a small child, my eyes were wide the whole time.

I spent some of my time writing poems and making up stories in my head. I daydreamed a lot, thinking about the "old timers," the miners who'd originally worked these creeks, and the unimaginable hardships they'd endured.

Those tough prospectors lived through the frigid winters, working frozen ground with nothing but their hands and the tools and supplies they could carry in.

I became fascinated with their stories and collected books about the Klondike, especially about the strong women who made their way north. Whenever I had a chance to fly into Dawson City or Whitehorse, I searched out more books and brought them back to camp.

A few women were mentioned over and over, and one became almost an obsession. Her name was Kate Rockwell, but she became better known as Klondike Kate or "the Belle of the Klondike."

I found Kate and her life so inspiring. She'd disguised herself as a boy to gain passage on a paddle-wheeler bound for Dawson, because women were not permitted. Like me, she was extremely daring but also naive—my spiritual doppelganger. When she arrived in the Yukon from New York City, she was only twenty, a singer, dancer and vaudeville entertainer determined to make something of herself. She was celebrated and remembered for her long red-gold hair, her verve and the memorable dances she choreographed and performed.

I read about these fascinating people whenever I had a few minutes to stretch and take a break from running equipment. I'd perch on a warm rock or a dry patch of hillside and read while swatting away the black flies and mosquitos.

I began to realize that Kate and I were alike in so many ways. I too was a rebel, leaving home when I was fifteen and running away often even before then. I was a dramatic child and could not stand authority. My mother and I were constantly at odds and fought daily. I was a handful, to be sure. Kate was the same—sent by her mother to convent school after convent school, thrown out of all of them because of her independent spirit.

Whenever the days were too long or the bears felt too close, I thought about Kate, and she reminded me of my own strength. Fortunately, it would be years before I understood just how much alike our lives would turn out to be.

I'd always dreamt of falling head over heels in love with a man who would accompany me on a life of travel and adventure. We would take our children with us on our journeys around the world—it was all I had ever longed for.

When I married Dean, I felt my real life had finally arrived.

As I mined for gold beside him, I thought a lot about Kate making a name for herself in Dawson City. Just like her, my dreams were finally coming true.

Dean also told me all kinds of stories about the gold rush—how, in the earliest days, miners scooped up buckets of gold from the riverbeds, limited only by how much they could carry.

Inside the bulldozer together, day after day, we talked and laughed and made plans for when we were rich—the grand house on the lake we would build, the sports cars we would drive.

He had a way of drawing me in. I listened attentively to his every word and dreamed of how amazing our life together would be. I believed everything he told me about travelling the world together and living our dreams. Some women fall for the way a man looks—I think I fell in love with Dean because of the way he dreamed. We were alike that way... nothing seemed impossible.

Our life on the creek was never boring, partly because we had so much work to do every day.

Each morning started with making sure that Maddy had everything she needed for the day: water, power, propane, supplies and wood for the fire.

We found an old wringer washer and Dean and Shawn dragged it to the main trailer. We set it up just inside the mudroom, close to the back door.

Maddy and I were so thrilled not to have to wash clothes by hand any more. The tub was soon filled with hot water and ready for its first load. We watched the rusty old tub swooshing clothes back and forth, back and forth, as the water turned dark muddy brown from the dirt. About ten minutes later, when the clothes looked as "clean" as the water, we drained the tub.

I began feeding one piece at a time through the wooden rollers.

Just as I was thinking that you wouldn't want to get your fingers caught because the rollers would break them in a second—my shirt sleeve caught. The roller drew it in, my hand drawn closer and closer. Just before anything truly disastrous could happen, Maddy grabbed my shirt sleeve with both hands and pulled as hard as she could, freeing me.

With the catastrophe averted, the whole situation became hilarious. Maddy's quick thinking and strength had saved me. (Which made me feel even worse later when I wasn't around to save her.)

As we stood beside the washtub, in ratty old clothes, hair all in knots, neither of us had had a proper shower in weeks. Maddy teased me about the silk pajamas I had in the washer. She said she thought I was "pretty fancy" bringing silk PJs to camp, and we giggled about it as I started to feed the beautiful eggplant-coloured top through the wringer. There was a loud, "Ping! Ping! Ping!" as the wooden rollers popped each button off my fancy pajamas, one at a time, ricocheting them around the mudroom like pretty little bullets.

I loved the life of a gold miner, even though I worked harder and longer hours than I'd ever imagined. Sometimes I was so exhausted I found a cozy spot in the nearest ditch to catch a few winks of sleep in the warm sun. Maddy and I had so much fun that first summer, and Dean and I fell more in love each day. Together almost twenty-four hours a day, we worked until we could barely stand and then drove the ATVs back to camp as fast as they would go, reaching speeds of sixty miles an hour.

Getting home first was a nightly competition. We tried to pass whenever we could squeeze by each other on the trails, the dust swirling behind us. It was not at all safe, but racing home gave us all something to look forward to at the end of the day.

We were reckless, never wearing helmets and having too much fun to care.

We saw so much wildlife in those days—some of the largest moose in the world live in the Yukon: surreal, massive creatures that tread majestically through the thick peat moss that blankets the land. Lynx, with their tufted ears and stocky boxer-like bodies. Coyotes, elk, caribou, wolves, foxes, beavers, martins—we often came across these and other unexpected companions.

One evening after a long day down at the claims, we rounded a corner and saw skid marks and broken ATV parts.

We slowed down, picking up the pieces.

As we bounced down the long hill leading to our camp, we could see the ATV we always left for Maddy. It was covered in mud and grass and its handlebars were flattened. The vinyl seat was torn and there were large dents on the fender and gas tank.

I raced inside to find out what had happened.

Maddy was on the sofa, wrapped in blankets, with an ice pack on her neck. Bursting into tears, she told me she'd decided to go down to the claims to surprise us with the fresh cinnamon buns she'd baked that morning. Rounding a sharp corner, she had seen a huge grizzly grazing beside the road just a few yards ahead.

Fight-or-flight kicked in, and her adrenaline-fueled first impulse was to try to scare it off by racing at it with the ATV. Thankfully, it worked, and the grizzly ran into the ditch and down the hill. But Maddy overshot the road, lost control of the machine, and rolled twice, end over end.

We couldn't figure out how she'd managed to get the ATV upright and drive it back. Her terror that the bear would smell the buns and come back gave her a surge of strength, enough to somehow wrestle the six-hundred-pound machine back on to its wheels and get back to camp and safety. Hours later, she was still shaking, and clearly in a lot of pain.

We all felt so badly that she'd had to go through that alone, but we were grateful, too, that she wasn't hurt even worse. It was a dose of Northern reality, our first real understanding of how serious even minor accidents can be in the wilderness. It would have taken at least a few hours to get a helicopter or airplane into camp—and that's if we had a satellite signal that day.

Not long afterward, Maddy decided to go home.

She was still in a lot of pain from the accident, and she'd had her fill of camp life. I was sad to see her go, but I understood.

Dean called on his Aunt Shelly to come and take Maddy's place as camp cook. She arrived not long after Maddy left, along with Ryan, an experienced excavator operator and pilot. He had his own bush plane, which was a huge bonus for us. We were a growing mining operation; at our busiest, we would employ twelve people.

I was soon running equipment all on my own. My first job was pushing dirt off the valley floor with the bulldozer, and for the life of me, I could not manage to make the ground level. Bulldozers have one very large blade at the front that can tilt up, down and side to side. It's used to push and simultaneously level the dirt as you go. If it worked, we would be able to drive the ATVs and trucks through the mining cut without getting stuck in the furrows.

I had a real problem with the leveling part. As I backed the machine up, it would buck up and down and throw me around the cab like I was on some sort of horrible carnival ride.

One day, Dean noticed that the bulldozer had stopped and came over to see what was going on. I looked at him with tears rolling down my dust-covered face.

"Do we have any dynamite? I need to blow this f'ing machine up!"

He chuckled and took pity on me, realizing a break was in order.

"Do you want to give the excavator a shot?"

I jumped at the chance. I was so done with that yellow hunk of metal. We switched machines and Dean gave me a few quick instructions.

At first it was doubly frustrating learning how to run a totally different machine, but after playing around with the controls for a few hours, I began to get the hang of it. From that point on, I was always in the excavator. I loved it! Within weeks, I was bailing dirt off the mining cut at a steady pace and was so proud of myself.

I became a skilled machine operator at Canadian Creek. When we first arrived, I wasn't sure what my role would be—I just happily followed Dean around, committed to being whatever he needed me to be. I did whatever I could at first, and as I learned more, I did more. I eventually mastered all the heavy equipment, including the bulldozers, rock trucks, excavators, sluice plants, and even the old Mac semi that we used to haul our fuel.

I took care of supplying the camp, and eventually took over as the person who picked up the fuel and supplies from the barge, too. The winding dirt road to the landing was long, rough and full of massive potholes. When it rained, it became a slippery, muddy mess. The creeks became so engorged that crossing them was a matter of life and death each time. I couldn't afford to be too cautious, because I was needed back at camp, but I also knew that many people had been swept away and drowned in similar situations. The price for being too brave was steep.

On one trip, it had been raining for days and Canadian Creek was raging. As I tried to make my way across, the force of the water pushed the tanker I was hauling sideways, the water crashing like ocean waves over the hood of the cab. I was terrified, but I was alone, and there was no choice but to keep pushing forward. The water flooded into the cab, and my feet were underwater on the gas pedal. There was a moment I was sure I would get pushed downstream with the truck if I didn't jump, but the weight and power of the old Mac somehow got us across. Once I reached the other side, I pulled over, taking deep breaths until I stopped shaking and could drive again.

I loved that truck, its little silver bulldog sitting proudly on the battered red engine hood.

Despite the terror I sometimes felt crossing the creeks, I looked forward to those trips. But eventually I was replaced on the fuel truck because I was needed more in the mine. Our whole operation depended on how many yards of dirt were sluiced through the massive plant, so I sat on the excavator seat all season long, moving dirt and loading rock trucks.

Dean and I always worked together, and whenever I needed help with something, I radioed him and he came over. As time went on, I needed less and less instruction and became much more confident in my abilities.

Later that summer, I also found the courage to operate the big bulldozer again and was proud of how efficient I became, finally mastering the art of pushing dirt while maintaining a level surface.

I was good enough that I sometimes graded the roads we

used each day. Keeping them in decent condition was critical for our mechanics and fuel trucks.

I often came across a lynx, bear or moose, and usually stopped to watch them, following at a respectful distance until they veered off the road and disappeared into the dense bush. Sometimes they would sit and watch me, staring me down.

Herds of caribou roamed the tundra, thousands of the regal animals moving together in perfect tempo. They were mesmerizing to watch. Coyotes and foxes ranged boldly around our camp, and we could often feel and hear wolves nearby.

And the bears were everywhere! And I do mean everywhere. I am absolutely terrified of them to this day.

I have my reasons.

CHAPTER FIVE

One beautiful summer day, we started working the ground early. I was in the bulldozer, slowly pushing dirt from the middle of the narrow valley to the outward edges of the cut. It was my job to do this all day, for about twelve hours, pushing the dirt and then backing up to fill my blade once again. It was boring, monotonous, and hard on the body, but my Sony Walkman helped make the days go faster. I sang at the top of my lungs, belting out my favourite songs. I often talked to myself, too, and practiced visualization techniques. I pictured where we would travel in the winters, and I built our lakeside home in my mind. I imagined the furniture we would choose and the cars we would buy, right down to their colour and upholstery.

We'd all learned that multiple mini-breaks for fresh air were essential for staying awake, and that day, Dean decided to surprise me with a picnic lunch. I looked down and saw him beside the tracks of my machine, a tiny bouquet of wildflowers in his hand.

We hiked into the forest, about a city block from our equipment, navigating over rocks, excavated boulders, gravel, dirt, broken tree roots and red clay.

The Yukon always seemed so green to me in summer. The moss that blanketed the forest floor was lush and dense, about two feet thick. Laying on it felt like being on a down-covered mattress.

There were very few large trees because the dirt was permanently frozen in most places, but wherever there was a patch of thawed ground, a few white spruce huddled together, competing for prime soil.

The woods were mostly made up of small birch trees, and they will always be my favourite. I could listen to the whispering sounds of the leaves in the wind for hours. Birch tree leaves are a brilliant green throughout the spring and summer; in the fall, they turn spectacular shades of orange, moody rusts and golden yellows. Hillsides are covered in these native trees, as far as the eye can see. It's a landscape forever etched in my mind.

We found a tree stump large enough to sit on to eat our lunch. Chatting about the morning's accomplishments and failures, I noticed that my shoulders were tense, and I could feel a familiar tightening in my temples. A migraine was trying to take hold, so I asked Dean to rub my shoulders. He stood behind me and I leaned back against his knees, closing my eyes and relaxing into his hands. Heaven.

Birds chirped on the forest floor around us as they searched for seeds and worms in the damp moss; an ever-so-slight breeze caught my hair and blew a strand across my cheekbone. Opening my eyes to push it off my face, I saw movement in the trees beside us.

Our minds process information quickly, and in a nanosecond my brain told me I was looking at a grizzly bear.

"BEAR!!!! Dean, BEAR!!"

I jumped up, knocking Dean backwards. He lost his balance just as I yelled, "Oh my god, three bears!"

The coat of the massive mama grizzly was so blonde it

looked white. The hair on the ridge of her back stood straight up, almost like a dog's when it's about to attack. She shook her huge head back and forth as she began to trot toward us.

It was a mother and her two-year-old cubs, two slightly smaller versions of her.

I think she smelled us before I even had the chance to stand up, because she was already picking up speed. There were only about forty feet between us.

Dean yelled, "RUN! RUN! RUN!" pushing me ahead of him at the same time.

I stumbled and fell. As I landed in the moss, I remembered what I'd been told: "Never run from a bear!"

My panicked mind froze, and it was all I could think: "Don't run, she will kill you if you turn your back."

Dean grabbed me by the back of my shirt, pulling me to my feet and again yelling at me to run, so I did. It was like a nightmare, though—the adrenaline made me feel like I was in slow motion, my heavy rubber boots filled to the top with cement.

Dean screamed into his handheld radio. "SHAWN, HELP, HELP, SHAWN HELP! We have a bear on top of us! LAY ON YOUR HORN!!!!!!"

I could hear the mama grizzly's laboured breathing right behind me. Every sound was amplified: each stick and branch breaking in her path, Dean's desperate calls for help, my own lungs gulping air. I prayed she wouldn't rip me to pieces and I wouldn't hear her massive jaws biting down on Dean's head, pulling him to the ground.

I was sure at least one of us was going to die there.

I broke suddenly through the wall of forest and fell into the mining cut. I forced myself not to look back, to keep running. I heard the bulldozer engine roar and saw Shawn in the cab ahead, the metal tracks crashing to the ground as he pushed it into high gear. Black smoke billowed into the blue sky, the colours strangely intensified and clear. I could see Shawn's face, his eyes wide as he pounded his fist onto the horn.

As I got closer, my legs collapsed and I fell to the ground. In what seemed like seconds, Dean was beside me and Shawn climbed down off the machine, screaming at us as he ran closer.

"Holy shit!!! That was the biggest fucking bear I have ever seen!"

Shawn said that when Dean called him on the radio, he looked up and saw us both running for our lives through the bush. All three bears had become confused when we rushed into the open cut and they heard the roar of the bulldozer.

They darted back and forth behind us before disappearing back into the dense forest.

I gasped for air, my legs shaking. I couldn't talk and tears ran down my cheeks. By some miracle, we had just outrun an eleven-hundred pound grizzly and her two giant sidekicks.

Dean and Shawn helped me up and all three of us started talking over top of one another, not quite believing what had just happened. The guys grabbed their guns and decided to go after the bears, fearing they'd be back sooner or later. I did not want them to go; I was terrified they would get hurt, but they insisted.

An hour or so later, they were back. They hadn't sighted the bears again, but they both said they'd never seen tracks as big as the ones the mama left behind.

We all knew that things would have turned out differently if we had been any further from Shawn and the Cat.

It was my first experience with grizzlies. It wouldn't be my last.

CHAPTER SIX

We knew we had to move our camp from the top of Casino Mountain to the valley where our claims were. We lost too much time each day riding the ATVs back and forth to work.

We began construction on a log home big enough to house twelve people, with a kitchen that could hold many weeks' worth of groceries and a table long enough for us all to sit at. Our camp crew was more like a large family and all our dinners were served family style. Everyone passed the potatoes and gravy and joked about the day's mishaps. We had some great laughs together.

We searched the hillsides for the largest trees we could find, tagged them with ribbon, and then cut them down, dragging them one by one to the site.

This was "after work" work. After our already long days, it was an exhausting job. Once we had logged every tree, we used the Cat and excavator to clear the site and then started to lay our foundation: a log skid built off the ground. In the spring the earth heaved with the melting permafrost, so the foundation had to be able to move with it.

Every log was painstakingly stripped of its bark by hand, using a wide, sharp metal blade with a wooden handle grip on either end. Each log rested on a large stump with massive spikes to stop it from rolling off.

I would start at the top of the tree and work my way to the bottom. Using short, quick pulling strokes, I yanked the blade through the thick bark, and it fell away to the ground. It was so hard, especially at first. If I didn't angle the blade just right, it jammed and stuck. Once I got the technique down and got into the rhythm, it went quite smoothly, but it was still grueling physical labour.

Plywood, framing wood and other building supplies had to be ordered from Whitehorse and Dawson City. Nails, insulation, flooring, windows, doors and roofing materials all came by barge down the Yukon River, where we collected it all with the Mac.

It was a huge undertaking, but we all loved seeing the astonished looks on people's faces when they flew into camp for the first time and saw a beautiful Whistler-style home in the middle of nowhere. Perched on the hillside overlooking our claims with its deep green metal roof, it really was a sight to see.

We were proud of it, and soon after, we built two smaller cabins, one for Dean and me and one for Shawn.

The upper floor of the house had five bedrooms and a living area with a large sectional couch and a TV. We had VHS movies and eventually we installed a satellite dish so we could even watch TV. I remember that day well—I was so excited to be able to watch the news and see what was going on at home. It felt like reconnecting with civilization.

We often had guests. Usually they were friends and family, but we had specialized equipment mechanics, geologists, pilots and hunters stay a night or two sometimes too.

My parents came for a visit one summer, and I was so eager to show them what we did for a living. It was much different to see how we lived in person rather than to hear about it through letters and pictures.

My dad was sixty-seven that year, and it was the first time he'd ever flown in an airplane, never mind a tiny four-seater.

They landed on the new airstrip we'd built on our Canadian Creek claims. We'd done our best, but that landing strip was dreaded by the bush pilots of the Yukon. It was short and rough—at one end was a solid wall of dirt, our tailings pile, and at the other was a dense wall of forest. The smaller planes had an easier time, but when we needed larger deliveries, the pilots did not look forward to landing at our site.

Pilots barely cleared the trees, sometimes scraping the belly of their planes hard as they flew over. Everyone on the ground clapped and cheered each time an airplane successfully lifted over the trees.

There was a strict weight limit—one too many suitcases or people could mean the end for them.

My sister Barb came to work for us as a cook one summer, too, and I went to Whitehorse to meet her at the airport. We flew back to camp in one of the smaller bush planes, bringing in groceries and a few parts.

Barb had never flown in a small plane, and she seemed excited. For the first hour, we talked a lot as I described everything to her: the names of each area we flew over, what type of animal was running through the bush below to escape us, and the names of the rivers and creeks we saw from the plane windows.

The flight was usually about two and a half hours. I loved being high in the air, but I was also nervous. Bush planes are so different from passenger jets—they're small, uncomfortable, loud and cold. The higher you climb, the colder it gets. Warm jackets and earplugs are essential. And turbulence in a bush plane is amplified; think of the worst turbulence you've experienced on a commercial flight and then multiply that by at least ten-fold.

Barb was in the back seat with me, and the seat beside the pilot had been removed to make room for groceries. Each box was fitted in like a puzzle piece, strapped down to keep it all from falling over. We did this to distribute weight, so it wasn't too heavy in the rear of the plane, making takeoff and landing a bit easier.

Each time we flew people and supplies into camp, the pilots would take the time to meticulously organize supplies, suitcases and passengers. Heavier people in the front, lighter in the rear. It was their responsibility to ensure we had a safe flight, so they took their time. Only when they were satisfied could we be on our way.

The turbulence on that flight was the worst I'd ever experienced, and I was uneasy. The clouds below us were becoming denser, making it difficult to see. The pilot decided to fly a bit higher and see if he could pop out of the cloud cover, but instead it became worse as we rose.

It felt like we were floating aimlessly in the sky for an eternity. I shut my eyes, only opening them when I started to feel dizzy. I wasn't sure if we were moving up or down. The clouds looked as thick as pudding.

Just as I felt panic rising, we burst out into the blue sky again. We had lost altitude and were now underneath the clouds. I was so relieved that we had made it through that I turned and gave my sister a huge smile.

My heart was beginning to beat at a normal rate again as I relaxed and took big, deep breaths. Then we slammed down hard, as if something had pulled the plane down. I grabbed on to the door beside me just as we slammed down again. The plane was flung to the left, then to the right. It listed back and forth while dropping hundreds of feet at a time, the force slamming us into our seats as if the laws of gravity and aerodynamics were overturned.

We could see the narrow valley where we had to land just ahead, the mountains looming high on both sides.

I clenched my eyes shut as hard as I could, grinding my teeth together as I prayed: *Please do not let this be my last day on Earth. Please.*

The turbulence continued relentlessly, and I looked ahead to see the pilot sit up as straight as he could, his back pushing hard against his seat. He sucked his stomach in, and, with his right hand wrapped tightly around the safety bar bolted to the centre of the dash, he cinched his seatbelt as hard as he could with his other hand. I could tell he was troubled, which did nothing to calm me. I shut my eyes once again, praying fiercely to God to please let us all live. I squeezed my eyes shut so hard that tears began to flow out of the corners and down my cheeks.

As instantly as it started, it stopped. We might have been driving a Cadillac sedan on an open highway.

I opened my eyes and looked over at my sister to see if she was okay. She looked at me with a big grin and gave me the thumbs up sign.

"Weren't you scared?" I yelled across.

She looked surprised. "No, was I supposed to be?" she said.

I burst out laughing. "YES, YES, YES!!! I thought we were going to die!"

I asked her later if she didn't once look over at me and see how frightened I was. She said that, because she had never flown in a small aircraft before, she thought our hellish rollercoaster ride was normal. She just kept looking out the window.

Just a few minutes after what felt like a near-death experience, the pilot made a beautiful landing.

The sun was shining, the sky was a brilliant azure blue, and the wind had become a warm, gentle breeze. Birds chirped as we exited the plane.

My legs felt like Jell-O and I couldn't stand, so I found a rock and sat down holding my head, giving my motion sickness some time to calm.

The pilot and I agreed it was the worst flight either of us had ever been on—we both felt incredibly lucky to have landed in one piece. He took his time before taking off again for Whitehorse.

CHAPTER SEVEN

One summer, we decided to stake another claim nearby. We knew we would run out of pay dirt on our site at some point, so we needed to secure new land to mine.

That summer was scorching hot and dry.

To sluice bedrock, our large shaker plant needed water. Lots of water. Hard rock mining extracts veins of gold from solid quartz rock; placer mining, the kind we did, mines gold that has already broken free from the quartz.

The gold we mined lay in the creek beds and channels, washed down to the valley floor sometimes hundreds or thousands of years before. We did not need to drill or blast; our seasons were spent stripping the valley of dirt, sometimes twenty, thirty or even forty feet of "overburden."

It could take months. After the ground had been stripped down to "paydirt," the substrate where gold might be found, we brought in our massive wash plant. We built a large, elevated pad made of overburden directly in front of the plant, long and wide enough to hold an excavator. The excavator fed paydirt into the hopper of the sluice plant. It was then "sluiced" (washed) in the hopper by twenty or thirty spray nozzles; the heavy gold finally washed into special mats designed to catch it.

Everything depended on the water we diverted from the creek.

To search for gold in the Yukon, you first have to buy, lease or stake claims. We chose to lease our claims on Canadian Creek from retired miners because they'd already been proven, meaning there were detailed reports on where gold lay heaviest in the valley. In addition to the initial cost of buying or leasing their claims, miners pay royalties to the claim owners, a percentage of the value of any gold that is mined.

Most miners either lease or buy claims. We couldn't afford to buy the claims outright at first, so leasing was our only option and we paid hundreds of thousands of dollars in royalties. Some claim owners fared better than the miners who leased and mined the valley, because mining is so costly.

Canadian Creek was laden with gold, and we mined about three thousand ounces each year, worth between five and six million US dollars in today's gold prices. Sadly, prices were much lower then—from 1998 through to 2001, gold averaged only $275 an ounce compared to today's price of $1,900 an ounce.

One warm day in August, Dean and I decided to hike over the hills to a nearby creek and stake virgin claims. He said it would be a short, half-day hike there and back.

I made sure we had lots of water and food for the day and were ready for anything the weather threw at us. We dressed in jeans, t-shirts, and runners. As we started out early in the morning, Dean wore a cozy, black and white sweater, and I had my light spring jacket and baseball cap. I carried a purple backpack with the lunches, drinks, toilet paper, black felt markers and a Sony Walkman with a few CDs. Dean's blue backpack held more water, a map, a foldable shovel to dig holes for our claim posts, and a small axe.

We set out right after a breakfast of waffles slathered in whipped cream with strawberries, telling the crew we were off on a hike for the day and to look for us if we didn't return. At the last moment, we decided to take Sam along too. Dean carried a rifle and some extra ammunition.

The morning climb was fairly easy, just a nice slow incline. We found some shade as the sun reached its peak and had our sandwiches, sharing a pop and a bottle of water.

The terrain grew steeper from there, the trees closer together and the underbrush denser. We were sweltering, so we drank more water. I was so hot that I finally stripped to my bra, underwear and runners. Dean laughed and decided to do the same. Stuffing our clothing into our backpacks, we had a great laugh at how it would look if we ran into someone, two people in their undies hiking deep in the middle of nowhere.

I was wearing out and asked how much farther we had to go.

"We should be able to see the creek soon," Dean said.

He was right. A few minutes further on, we came out of the trees onto its dry bed. I still don't know how he managed to find it without a compass or anything other than an old map, but he did.

To make our claim, we had to chop down a few skinny trees for posts a minimum of five inches in diameter; they had to stand at least four feet above ground. The posts had to be flattened on two sides, so Dean used his axe to scrape the bark off. With our black marker, we wrote the claim name, the length of the claim, the date and my full name on those sides.

My very own claim! I was ecstatic

We then had to pound the posts into the ground—the claim would only last as long as they stood.

Afterward, we rested and had a picnic, celebrating over the rest of our sandwiches and the fruit and brownies I'd packed. We were both starving and gobbled everything up as fast as we could, keen to start back down the mountain. It was late afternoon when we headed down—the trip in and the staking had taken longer than Dean had guessed, but we still had lots of daylight ahead.

I mentioned that we needed to find a creek with water—we'd already drunk every drop we'd brought along.

The bright blue sky started to cloud over not long after we set out, making it darker under the trees. I was soon back in my clothes and happy I had brought a jacket.

We walked for what seemed like forever, eventually coming across what should have been a flowing creek. It was totally dried up—it had been such a dry summer that all the small creeks had vanished.

I asked how much longer it would take to get back to camp. I was especially worried for Sam, as he hadn't had any water or food since we left early that morning.

Dean didn't answer right away.

"Are we lost?" I asked. I had such faith that Dean knew what he was doing, always, that I hadn't considered the possibility until that moment.

"No—I know where we are," he said, holding up his trusty map. But as the hours rolled by and he continued to tell me we weren't lost, I feared we were absolutely lost. I felt panic rising in my chest. There were thousands of square miles of nothing but bush between us and the nearest town. If we were lost, what were the chances of being found?

But I didn't tell Dean how frightened I was, and he kept reassuring me we would make it home before dark.

I trusted him.

When the bright daylight began to fade, it became too dangerous to keep walking. Dean used a couple of his bullets to shoot into the air in case the crew had come looking for us, but no one came.

We knew we needed to find a place to shelter and try to keep warm. Even in the heat of summer, the temperature fell quickly at night. We found a low spot and huddled together on the mossy forest floor. Dean curled up behind me and I managed to get Sam to lie in front of me. I cuddled in between the two of them.

It felt like Sam knew we needed him to lie with us. His instinct was to help keep me warm and I think he sensed we were in danger. The temperature dropped to just above freezing on the hills that night; Sam helped us avoid hypothermia.

I was so cold I didn't sleep, and I kept hearing things move in the dense bush. I was terrified a bear would come across us—between fear and the cold, I shook uncontrollably for those few hours of night.

When there was enough light to see a few feet in front of us, we started out again. We had no idea where we were at this point and looked for another creek, even a dry one, to follow down to the valley floor.

As we walked, I looked for a clearing, hoping we could get into the open and get our bearings, maybe even see something familiar. But that never happened. The forest was so thick we could barely walk at all, and sometimes we crawled under the brush on our hands and knees.

I was so thankful I worked out regularly and was in good shape. There is no way I would have been able to cover so many miles of tough terrain otherwise.

By mid-afternoon, I'd again removed everything but my underwear and bra to try to keep cool. I didn't think about it at the time, but we were burning precious calories and becoming more and more dehydrated. My lips were cracked and my feet ached and burned.

I was now in full panic mode. It's terrifying to understand you are lost in hundreds of square miles of wilderness and nobody knows where you are.

My panic made me feel that if we stopped, we would never make it home, so I became robotic, walking faster and faster, pushing my way through sharp branches that scraped my face, arms and legs. My hands bled from grabbing at tree branches to pull myself over uprooted trees and stumps.

"I feel like we are travelling in circles," I said.

"No, we're headed in the right direction," he replied.

Just to be sure, as he walked ahead of me, I tied a chunk of toilet paper to a tree branch, and then a few more along the way. I thought it might help if a search crew came looking for us, too.

By late afternoon, Dean's knee hurt badly and he needed to rest for a bit. We found a log to sit on and something caught my eye in the distance—a toilet paper strip I had tied to a tree hours before.

I felt the bottom of my stomach fall out.

"We are one hundred percent lost," I blurted, feeling panic rising.

I had no idea which way to go. Should we stay put? Was anyone looking for us? What were the chances of them finding us? Fearful thoughts flooded my mind. I think I'd been trained to be afraid—the stories I'd heard of people being lost in the North never ended well.

Dean came over and put his arms around me, pulling me close and just letting me freak out for a bit.

After a few minutes, he said, "Don't worry. I will get us home, I promise."

I tried to have faith in him, but it wasn't easy after spending twenty-four hours walking in circles.

Eventually we started out again, Dean out in front. I kept turning back to see if Sam was okay—he was usually always in front of us, leading the way, but on this trip, he kept dragging behind. I was worried about him. We all needed water. I licked my cracked lips and was shocked. Touching them with my fingertips, I found deep crevices splitting my skin. I also had blisters on my toes and the leather of my shoes had rubbed my heels raw.

Dean's knee was so painful he soon sat down to rest it again. I sat beside him and pulled off my runners. My white socks were soaked with blood, so I carefully rolled them off. Underneath, my toes had huge, weeping blisters and my ankles were raw and bleeding. It was excruciating sliding my shoes back on over my oozing wounds.

This isn't good, I thought. Soon I won't be able to walk at all. Dean was in even worse condition than me.

As we walked aimlessly through the trees, Sam suddenly veered to the right, and then stood still, watching us. He barked as if he wanted our attention. I had an overwhelming feeling that he wanted us to follow him.

"I want to follow Sam," I said. He was part St. Bernard, after all, a breed famous for its rescue abilities. I remembered hearing that they had an uncanny sense of direction.

Dean resisted, but I refused to follow him any longer.

"I'm sticking with Sam, Dean—with or without you." I stomped off and he followed grumpily.

Sam crisscrossed the hill and then started down a steep gorge. We navigated a rocky ledge that led us to an open hillside. Ahead of me by about thirty feet, Dean yelled out—he could see the mining cut! Although it was far in the distance, it was hard to miss, the mass destruction an ugly sight. But at that moment, it was the prettiest thing I had ever seen. I started screaming and jumping up and down.

"We found it, we found it!"

As we hugged, I started to cry, overcome with relief.

We continued to follow Sam, and he eventually led us past every piece of toilet paper. I realized that he had been trying to help us all along. No wonder he'd walked behind us.

It took another five hours or so to finally make it back to camp. By the time we did, Dean was crawling behind me. As I limped up the stairs, Sam reached the open screen door before me and barked. Our cook Shelly came running down and said the guys were out looking for us; she had been just about to call search and rescue on the satellite telephone.

Dean collapsed onto an old wooden bench, extending his leg out in front of him to ease the pain in his knee. The last bit of adrenalin left my body and I slumped onto the plywood floor. Shelly brought me a pillow and blanket. I could barely keep my eyes open and sat up only to drink a jug of water that she brought for each of us.

I asked her to get water and food for Sam and then make Dean and me something to eat.

It is still one of my favourite memories of our time at Canadian Creek: sipping chicken noodle soup out of a cup, biting into the best grilled cheese sandwich I had ever tasted, lying on the porch with a down-filled pillow under my head and a fluffy quilt covering me up to my neck. After that, I don't remember anything for a few hours. I was woken later by the sound of the crew happily talking to Dean.

That feeling of pure thankfulness and joy has never left me.

When I remember that time, the time I sank to the porch floor in utter exhaustion and relief, I can smell the chicken noodle soup steaming in its mug. It is still the most comforting smell I know.

I am convinced Sam saved us that day. He was the most wonderful dog, and he stayed beside us for about five more years. I sobbed when he could no longer walk on his own and the vet had to put him down.

To me, Sam was "the Great Wonder Dog of the Yukon Territory." We were heartbroken when he left us in 2005.

May you forever rest in peace in Doggie Heaven, Sam.

CHAPTER EIGHT

I loved the gold-mining life.

It always created excitement when people found out what we did for a living, and they had so many questions.

Dean loved the admiration, respect and power that came with gold mining and would sometimes casually pull a bag of nuggets out of his pocket at the hardware store or in a restaurant. People often thought the gold was fake until he let them hold it—then you could see the contagious excitement in their faces.

There is something about raw gold. The colour, feel and sheer weight of it is mesmerizing.

Gold fever: it lures you in and casts its spell on you.

Every day, I collected nuggets from the sluice plant, some big, some small. We filled our pockets. It's hard to describe the intoxication of knowing our plant would hold tens of thousands of dollars in gold at the end of each day. It made us want to work harder and longer.

I grew up during those years in the Yukon, and developed confidence I'd never had before. It felt as if people admired me—they certainly treated me differently than they treated Brandee, the young waitress. It was a feeling I treasured, something I had been looking for my whole life. Being gold miners made us feel a tiny bit like celebrities.

One spring, on a whim, we decided to participate in an international gold and gem show in Salt Lake City before heading back to our claims. We registered by telephone, clueless about what to expect.

Dean built a display box out of old pieces of stained wood and filled it with rocks and sand. Over the years, I'd collected miniature diecast metal replicas of our equipment: bulldozers, excavators, rock trucks and loaders. We created a simulation of our mining claims by meticulously arranging each piece of equipment inside the box. The detailed designs of the cabs, exhaust stacks, and individually linked metal tracks brought the scene to life. We also bought a VCR and a small TV to play video we had captured over the years of us mining. And we brought raw gold, of course. Lots of it. We had nuggets of all sizes, some made into pendants by a jeweller friend. We displayed the nuggets on plush green velvet, arranging five tiny spotlights above them to enhance their shine. I filled small glass vials with gold dust, hoping to sell them by weight.

The drive was about fifteen hours and we arrived late at night, falling into our hotel bed. The next morning, after a quick shower and a drive-through breakfast, we checked into the gold show, pulling our vehicle to the side door as directed.

I wanted Dean to go in first to find our booth location, but he insisted I go while he unloaded.

I nervously opened the door and peeked inside. I couldn't believe how many vendors were already set up. Making my way down the first aisle, I noticed that the displays were extremely professional. As I searched for our location, it was clear that we were way out of our league—this was a jewellery convention!

Why didn't I research this more?!

My anxiety intensified as I hurried past beautiful glass displays of sparkling diamond rings, others dripping with gold necklaces, earrings and bracelets.

I finally located our exhibitor spot and hurried back to the loading zone. Throwing the door open to find Dean standing with our TV and crusty wooden box, I blurted, “We are so screwed!”

I was in a cold sweat, and hyperventilating slightly.

“We cannot go in there! It’s a jewellery exhibition, not gold.” I was so embarrassed. “We can’t set this up. The whole place will be laughing at us.”

“We are not going home,” Dean replied, his trademark smile in place. “We came all this way. Let’s just be brave and do it.”

We started laughing at the complete ridiculousness of our situation.

As we walked by each glittering display, I noticed that everyone else was dressed formally. The women were in dresses or skirts and high heels; the men all wore shirts, ties and slacks. I was mortified. In our jeans, runners and T-shirts, I felt like everyone was looking at us.

Could this get any worse?

By the time we reached our booth location, I couldn’t stop giggling. Dean pointedly gave me his, “For the love of God, will you please shut up?!?” look.

We managed to find a plug for our TV, and I hurriedly assembled the video set-up and pushed play. Our booth had two tables that we set up in an L-shape, with information on our mine and our location in Canada on one end. Even in my mortified state, I thought the miniature claim display looked great. Next to it were the gold nugget pendants and vials filled to the brim with fine gold. We scattered thousands of dollars’ worth of various-sized nuggets on the velvet. The "pièce de resistance" was a huge, ten-ounce nugget the size of my palm.

The videos showed images of us running equipment and the sluice plant in operation, explaining how we stripped the dirt and pushed it off the cut with the help of massive bulldozers and excavators, and how we sluiced the paydirt and retrieved the gold.

There was soon a small crowd gathered to watch the screen, and the rest of the day went by in a blur. At times we had people crowded five or six deep, straining to see the TV and to get close enough to see a glimpse of our raw gold.

I was stunned by the commotion at our little display—even the other vendors took turns coming by. Dean and I answered so many questions that we both lost our voices by the end of the day.

We'd hoped we would sell enough gold dust and nugget pendants to pay for our trip, and we sold every speck of gold we brought with us. We had so much cash that I couldn't even close the briefcase I kept it in. We laughed and laughed—it was the opposite of what we'd expected to happen once we realized what we'd gotten ourselves into.

We had the best time on that trip, solidifying our ten minutes of fame.

During the mining season, we often had hundreds of thousands of dollars' worth of gold scattered around our camp kitchen, sealed in bags, or sitting on plates waiting to be weighed and cleaned. Nuggets were stored in large plastic peanut butter jars we saved for that reason. Eventually it was all dropped off at the refiner to be smelted and deposited into our metal account.

I had a stunning collection of beautiful necklaces, bracelets and earrings made of gold from our claims.

We saved all our best nuggets to bring to one of the many

jewelry stores in Dawson or Whitehorse. They loved them, as the purity of our gold was high, and they crafted beautiful jewelry to sell to the tourists who flocked to the Yukon every summer. Nuggets fetched a much higher price than fine gold, and our creek produced a lot of these rarities.

Some miners flaunted huge gold nugget inlaid belt buckles, watch bands and rings on every finger. We were our own unique community, for sure. We all wanted bragging rights for the most gold produced that year.

With its wide dirt streets and rows of bars and casinos, Dawson still resembles the city it was back in the 1890s. The music in Diamond Tooth Gertie's dance hall plays on, with can-can dancers and lots of drunken miners throwing money around long into the night.

Whenever we were there, I imagined Kate Rockwell making her fortune, miners coming from many miles away to watch her dance and hear her laugh. I could feel her there, and I knew that we were somehow connected, two links in a long chain of women who refused to settle for the life they were first handed.

Dawson is still a city of wanderers, gold-seeking men and women—lots of huge hearts and more than a few liars, thieves and scoundrels.

In the winters, Dean and I took expensive vacations to places like the South of France, Belgium, New Zealand, Hawaii and Mauritius—all the beautiful experiences money could buy.

Our multimillion-dollar house on the lake shore sat on sixty acres. When we weren't traveling, our winters were spent skiing local mountains and riding brand new snowmobiles and ATVs. We threw lots of lavish parties for friends and family.

Dean had promised me that my dreams would come true, and they did. Our hard work together in the North had paid off—we were living a life that most people could only dream of. Not surprisingly, our friends and relatives thought we had it all.

The truth was that Dean and I had both changed. I'd grown up and become more confident—he had everything he'd dreamed of, and found he wasn't satisfied. His discontent turned into rage, and more and more often, he was turning that rage toward the people who loved him the most.

When I looked in my eyes in the mirror after the first few years of our marriage, it was sadness I saw, but I did everything I could to keep it hidden. Who was going to feel sorry for the poor little rich girl? And I loved our life most of the time. I had learned to be afraid of Dean, and yet I hadn't stopped loving him.

I fought hard to keep us on track, to forgive him when he belittled me. I felt like a terrified puppy protecting my exposed belly, trying my hardest to be good and not provoke him.

We'd often go for months without an incident, and we still had so much fun during those times. Then the pressure would get to him again, and I would somehow accidentally push the wrong button.

When I felt the most helpless, I found hope in my daydreams, often pretending I was the Belle of the Klondike, Kate herself. She went through terrible times because of the man she loved too. But there was one enormous difference between her life and mine—I knew how hers ended. It was a comfort to me on the hardest days. If Kate could make it through, so could I.

CHAPTER NINE

Kate

My mother came from nothing. But she was beautiful, and she would not let a little thing like poverty stop her from becoming the lady she knew herself to be. When I was born in Junction City, Kansas, in 1876, Mother was a waitress, and my father worked on the railroad. When I was five, my mother came into her own, divorcing my father and marrying the most successful man in town—her lawyer, Carl.

We moved to Spokane, where Carl soon became a successful judge. We lived in a fine manor, with servants and a governess to keep me out of the way. My stepfather was kind and "spoiled" me, at least according to my mother. I grew up playing hooky from school to go fishing, camping and riding with him when I wasn't practicing my singing and dancing.

Not surprisingly, because I looked just like my mother had at my age, I drew the attention of the gentlemen. By the time I turned thirteen, the way my stepfather's friends and colleagues looked at me enraged her, and she sent me off to boarding school, first in Kansas, then in Minnesota, and finally in California, all with the same dismal results. I learned a lot because I was a quick study, but the nuns and I were oil and water.

When I was sent home from California, I found that disaster had struck my family. The country was in a depression, and my stepfather had somehow managed to lose almost everything. My mother was unhappy, to say the least, and another divorce soon followed.

She and I headed for South America on an eighty-seven-day cruise. It sounded like a grand adventure, and I was thrilled to be at sea.

By then I was sixteen, and I had blossomed: I was a natural redhead with violet eyes, rare in those days, and had my mother's curvy hourglass figure and long legs. But I think it was my nature that was most attractive to the young men—I loved to laugh, and when I did, it seemed as if everyone except my mother laughed with me. I was the belle of the ship and captured the attention of the young naval officers on board. Two months into our trip, I surprised Mother with my engagement to a particularly handsome officer.

Regrettably, she didn't see it as the success I did, and to my horror, she chased him off with threats of a lawsuit. A few ports later, she stuck me in a Catholic convent school in Valparaiso, Chile. She then headed off on what I would later learn was a romantic adventure of her own. Sadly, my mother was losing her touch, or perhaps just her youth. Her tryst with the wealthy traveller would turn out to be just that, a tryst.

Eventually Mother returned to New York, just in time to receive a letter from the nuns in Valparaiso. They informed her that I had evaded my chaperones long enough to become engaged again, this time to a young military diplomat from Spain.

Ever jealous of my happiness, or perhaps thinking I was too young to marry, Mother ordered me home. After a hair-raising trip around Cape Horn and another ninety-seven days at sea with the worst storms I'd ever experienced, I landed back in the US.

Needless to say, I hated her with all my heart.

Then I found out that things were even worse than I'd thought. Much worse. Mother needed me home to work. I was now eighteen, and she had somehow squandered every last penny she'd wrung from my stepfather. She was destitute, and with her looks fast fading, I was her only hope.

She worked at a shirt factory and wanted me to join her there, but in the newspaper, I spotted an ad that read: "Chorus girls wanted, no experience necessary." Well, I thought, if I had to work, I would use my natural assets.

I applied for the job and was told I was "a natural," which I believe meant I was young, pretty, curvy and willing to bare my legs and decolletage.

My first appearance as a page girl at a Coney Island honky-tonk went well, and I quickly graduated to the chorus line. The moment I knew what I was doing, I moved up: New York's vaudeville theatres!

Yet the real money, I'd heard, was not in New York at all, but out West. I was offered a job back in Spokane, and there, between my earnings for dancing and the tips, I was able to start saving even while supporting Mother.

On the street, it was still considered appalling to show one's ankles, but in the theatres, our daring costumes displayed much more. Men seemed powerless to hang onto their money when tempted by an innocent face on a scantily costumed dancer.

I was happy in Spokane, but then we began to hear about the Klondike. It was the beginning of the second huge North American gold rush, one that was rumoured to make the California gold rush look parsimonious by comparison.

I packed my things, said goodbye to Mother, and headed for Alaska. The trip was long and often rough, but after my wild trip around the Cape, I felt ready for anything. I found a job at a saloon in Juneau called the Louvre the same day I arrived—it was the only place in town that didn't require its entertainers to continue to "entertain" in the rooms upstairs after the shows.

A few months later, I was able to buy a place on a ship heading north to Skagway, where I joined the chorus at the infamous Soapy Smith's honky-tonk, Jeff. Smith's Saloon. It was not easy to maintain my virtue while maximizing tips in these places, but I found that I'd learned a lot from my mother about how to manage men. Never would that knowledge be more useful than during my years in the Klondike.

It was terribly expensive getting from one place to another in the North, but I was finally able to save enough money to board the train from Skagway to Lake Bennett.

I admit I was starting to get impatient, determined as I was to make it to the gold fields and the real money. I was never going to find myself in my mother's situation—I would make my own wealth.

I felt much closer to my goal in Bennett, which was not more than a camp itself. This was the gateway to the Klondike, and its business was getting men on the trail. I was the only performer at the old Bennett Hotel, and I often danced and sang all night, putting on as many as twenty shows a day.

I would make it to Dawson City, the heart of the Klondike, whatever it took. It was all we talked about, because that was where my customers were heading too. We dreamed together, describing the houses we'd build and the European capital cities we'd travel to once we'd made it big.

One night, not long after I arrived, some of the would-be miners insisted on nailing my name in champagne corks to the ceiling of one of the shoddy rooms upstairs. The myth was that anyone sleeping in the room would dream of me. I took it all in good grace, of course, but I couldn't help but think that I would soon have my name in lights over much larger and more luxurious rooms.

Finally, in June of 1900, I had enough money saved to leave for Dawson City. So many men had frozen or starved to death on the trails that the RCMP insisted on checking each person's gear to make sure they had the means to make it. But I had another obstacle to overcome—my skirts. I had paid for a place on a boat bound for the Klondike, but the Mounties would not allow a woman onboard.

When I realized that my charm wasn't going to make my case for me—that in fact it seemed to make the officer even more protective—I knew I'd have to find another way. For a few dollars I was able to purchase a worn pair of pants and a shirt from one of the smaller men, along with a felt cap to tuck my hair under. Binding my chest with a scarf and rubbing some dirt on my face as a disguise, I snuck past the policeman and onto the wharf. There, I found I was too late—the boat had already cast off. I was so close to getting out of Bennet, and I couldn't let anyone stop me.

Crying out "Whoop! Whoop!" to get the attention of the men on board, I ran and leapt from the dock and hit the water. I'd never learned to swim, so I had a good incentive to grab the line that had just been untied from the dock, and the men quickly pulled me aboard.

My cap was still in the lake, and my red hair, now dripping wet, fell loose for the Mountie on the dock to see.

"Return to the dock right now!" he bellowed, but he was too late. The boat kept moving and there was no way for him to come after us.

We were on our way to Whitehorse. The Mounties didn't get "their man" that day!

We made it through the rough waters of the Five Finger Rapids, and a few hours later, to the most treacherous part of our journey, Miles Canyon.

Soaring cliffs on either side of the river forced its waters into a channel a third of its usual width and our captain navigated the boat through what felt like a rock funnel. The gentle river was transformed into a wild, hazardous force, tossing the boat and everyone on it like so many children's toys.

Having made it so far and worked so hard, I was not afraid. I knew I was meant to reach the Klondike and make my fortune, and so I felt only excitement. As the men around me grew pale, I tried to hide my happiness, but the truth is that I had never felt quite so alive in my life.

I must report that Dawson was initially a disappointment. I expected reasonably comfortable accommodations here in the heart of the gold fields. But perhaps because it was so costly to ship supplies and everything else here, the "city" was mostly just a large, dirty and overpopulated campground.

It took me only a few hours to find a job at the Savoy Theatrical Company, where I was billed as a "Soubrette Extraordinaire."

I learned quickly that having to earn my way to Dawson had given me a huge advantage—unlike the performers fresh in from Seattle or San Francisco, I already knew what the miners needed. I knew how to make them forget their troubles and focus on their dreams. The Savoy had been closed by a fire, and I was thrilled to be its headliner when it reopened. We had a full house and great reviews immediately. The local broadsheet reported that, wearing a rose-coloured, lace-trimmed ball gown and a Lillian Russell hat trimmed with colourful ostrich plumes, I wowed the audience of mostly men with my charisma and happy-go-lucky style.

The unkempt and homesick miners seemed to be happiest listening to the old songs, favourites like "Sweet Rosie O'Grady" and "Put Your Arms Around Me, Honey."

It wasn't long before they were calling me "Klondike Kate," and I had gained modest fame. (I wasn't the first Klondike Kate—she was a miner from Atlantic Canada. But I was honoured to have my name linked to the place that made so many rich anyway, and the sobriquet would serve me well throughout my life.)

There were so many memorable characters in the Yukon, and it wasn't long before I met Arizona Charlie Meadows, who'd built the lavish Palace Grand Theatre. He was tall and looked the part of a showman, his long hair reaching past his shoulders under a broad-brimmed hat. I never saw Charlie without his fringed buckskin jacket and signature red bandana tied jauntily around his neck.

One night after a particularly successful show at the Savoy, when I was called back for encore after encore, Charlie approached me quietly.

"Kate, you should come to the Grand. I'll triple your pay, and you can have the Stars Suite."

I'd heard of this beautiful suite, which looked out over Front Street from the second floor, spacious and furnished as finely as any Seattle hotel.

How could I say no?

The Grand Palace was a landmark, built from the lumber of two abandoned sternwheelers. It was three stories, the interior lined with horseshoe-shaped balconies on the second and third floors. These were private boxes used by the wealthiest of its patrons. There was also a saloon and gaming halls, and of course, my new suite, its interior papered in flocked red and gold, matching the lush red carpet. By the window was a rocking chair where I could watch people coming and going on the busy street below as I dreamt up my new performances. I could even see the Yukon River—I wrote Mother to tell her all about it, but I longed to be able to have her here to show her what I'd accomplished with only my talents. Who needs a husband??! Her experiences had taught me that independence was essential, and here I was, living in style and earning more than most people in trousers.

Charlie was impressed by my choreography and encouraged me to do more, to create a performance that audiences would never forget. I did, but first I used some of the skills the nuns had beaten into us to sew more than two-hundred yards of yellow, orange and red chiffon into a long train that danced like flames as I twirled my hips and a cane. The dance I created was a stunning spectacle, and at the end I collapsed gracefully to the floor, swallowed by the fire I'd created.

Until the evening I first performed that dance, I think even Dawson City could have forgotten me when I left. That night, as the men leapt to their feet, stamping and clapping and shouting my name, I knew that I would be remembered. I had instantly become a celebrity.

I was twenty-four when I walked onto that stage, covered in red sequins and glittering rhinestones, my long legs flattered by racy pink tights. Everyone in the audience fell quiet as I stood still, gazing intently into the darkened room. The squeaking chairs and clinking bottles hushed. It seemed as if the entire room waited for me, even the lumber of those old paddle wheelers. The anticipation was electric, and before it could make me nervous, I slipped the satin cape that covered my curve-hugging costume off my shoulders and onto the floorboards. With my arms outstretched, as if reaching for someone to keep me tethered to the Earth, I floated about the stage.

Offstage, a violin cut the silence, its keening notes troubling the air, sending tremors into the marrow of the men in those seats.

I began to twirl, holding the cane high in the air, the fabric lifting upwards, creating the illusion of flames. In a rising tide of crimson and gold, I leapt and twisted, lifted by the ethereal music as it drove me to move faster and faster, the stage now a sea of fire.

We could all feel the heat, and I could see the light of the fire in the mesmerized faces of the men in the front row. Finally, my entire body damp, I sank to the floor, and the chiffon drifted slowly down around me like dying embers.

My newly smitten fans jumped to their feet, and I looked up to see them throwing bags of gold dust, nuggets and gold coins onto the stage, their faces wild with joy.

When the curtain fell each night, it was time to change and mingle with my patrons. An eleven-piece orchestra played waltzes and polkas; for just a dollar, the men could buy a dance with me. Afterwards, I entertained them at the bar, listening raptly to their jokes and stories, earning a 25 percent commission on each drink they ordered.

My mother had earned less than eight dollars a week, working twelve hours a day, six days each week. I earned two hundred dollars a week in salary, but my tips and commissions topped

$750 many nights. Watching Mother with my stepfather had taught me to listen well— sympathetically, tenderly and with sincere interest. It wasn't long before those skills, along with my talents, had earned me enough money to set Mother up in comfort for the rest of her life. It gave me pleasure, not all of it virtuous, to care for her so well when she had cut me to the quick by sending me away as a girl.

My youth had been short on affection, and it was impossible not to be moved by the attention, compliments and gifts I received from the miners.

Dawson City was a world of paradox. For example, on Christmas Eve in the first year of the twentieth century, 1900, I wore a fifteen-hundred-dollar ivory satin Parisian gown. The miners crowned me the "Queen of the Yukon," fashioning a rough crown out of an old tin can. They placed fifty small lit candles on its jagged edges, and I danced under it carefully, wax dripping into my long, thick braids.

I was showered with adoration, but that night, I felt strangely drawn to the one man who seemed not to notice me. John Matson sat by himself, off in a corner. I went over and did my very best to draw him out, but he could barely choke out a few words, and his heavy Norwegian accent made even those difficult to understand. I finally gave up and returned to the fray. I had no idea that, decades later, those few minutes would bring me many years of happiness.

By the end of the first year, I'd made more than thirty thousand dollars. In addition to ensuring that my mother was well looked after, I imported a wardrobe of handmade French lingerie and the finest dresses. But most of my earnings were kept at Dawson's only bank, ready to build my mansion and fund my world travel when my work here was done.

The streets of Dawson were not paved with gold, as rumour had it down south, but the gleaming metal was everywhere else—in the pockets of men in the saloons, on the boats headed south, and laying heavy in the creeks, just ready for harvest. The men treated me like the queen of it all.

I loved my life in Dawson, even buying a dog sled team so I could fly behind them down the frozen Yukon River. Often after we finally shut down the bar for the night, I'd sit by my window and watch the magical aurora borealis stream through the darkness. In the warmer months, I rode my horse Bly as often as I could, often rising early to leave Dawson behind, riding for miles through the surreally beautiful countryside.

Even so, I was lonely. My relationship with the miners was a delicate one—I could be loved by them all as long as I didn't pay special attention to any one of them. I was fine with that, and good at it, if I do say so myself. Watching my mother fade away after my stepfather lost everything had not endeared me to tying myself to one man.

But it was loneliness that tempted me into conversation with the poorest man in the Palace one night, the lowly bartender. In a city full of unkempt, bearded men, I must say that his smooth-shaven face was attractive in a startling way. He wasn't handsome, and he wasn't tall, but Alexander Pantages had a way of seeming as if he were in charge even as he poured drinks for miners. He was also twenty-four that year, and I soon found his dark eyes mesmerizing. The look in them told me that we were alike in dreaming huge dreams.

As we talked, that night and many others, I learned that his blinding drive to succeed was even stronger than my own. His passion was the theatre—he loved the excitement of the stage. He was illiterate and had been raised in brutal poverty, working from the age of nine as a busboy and later as a waiter in Cairo until he managed to escape his authoritarian father, signing up as a cabin boy on a French steamship. He eventually made it to San Francisco, where he became a prize fighter and worked in theatres. Like me, he'd come north to accumulate real wealth, the kind that bought freedom and respectability.

I was entertained and impressed by his stories about how he'd finally made it to Dawson City.

He'd landed in Skagway with just a pair of boots wrapped in the Seattle Post Intelligencer and twenty-five cents in his pocket. He had no idea how he'd earn the money for the next leg of his journey and was looking for any work at all when someone on the street called out, "I'll give you five dollars for that newspaper!"

Another man yelled, "I'll give you ten!"

Thinking quickly, Alexander replied, "Not for sale." He then rented a hall on spec, promising the owner a share of his profits and the newspaper after he was finished. Selling tickets for a dollar per person to the news-starved community, he hired a man to read out each of the articles, one after another.

He earned enough to make his way to Dawson City, where he found a lucrative job as a bartender for Arizona Charlie. Alexander quickly realized that he could let the miners work hard for the gold; he'd get it from them the easy way.

Soon after I first introduced myself, Alexander began to assist me in relieving drunks of their gold after the show. He'd nod toward the most generous, and he had a hand sign for those who were rude and deserved to be charmed out of the largest possible sum.

It wasn't too long before I realized I was in trouble. It was

Alexander who I thought about as I was falling asleep, and it was his laugh I listened for when I said something clever. Before I had time to think about what a terrible idea it was, Alex had become the focus of my life.

Even so, I managed to keep our relationship to friendship until one night Charlie's prize-winning fighter failed to show up. That was when Dawson City, Charlie and I all learned that Alexander had fought welterweight in San Francisco. The match was sold out, and he made short work of his opponent, knocking him out within the first few minutes of the fight. But I'd been so afraid for him that later, when we were alone after the theatre closed, I couldn't keep myself from leaning so close that it could only be an invitation to a kiss. When he finally drew back, my breath drawn deep into his lungs and his into mine, I knew I would follow Alexander Pantages anywhere.

Charlie gave him a ten percent interest in his shows out of gratitude for his boxing win, and Alexander very quickly became his stage manager.

I fell more and more crazy in love. Have you ever thought about how it's referred to as "falling" in love? That should have been a clue, even if I'd forgotten everything I learned from my mother about the importance of independence. I fell, alright.

One night, jealous of the miners who regularly tried to convince me to marry them, Alexander had a bit of a tantrum. He said that he had to stop seeing me, that it killed him to pretend to be nothing but a friend. He wanted our relationship out in the open, and in the absence of a minister, that meant living with him and working beside him. I was afraid, of course, but deep down, all I'd ever wanted was the love of someone who wanted only to be with me while we became very rich and travelled the world.

Our first official project together was the old Orpheum, a theatre that had opened and closed quickly before slipping into disrepair. We bought it using some of my savings and worked hard to resurrect it into a showpiece. (Alexander said that his savings were earmarked for our first theatre in Seattle, so I could hardly argue.)

One day my friend Isobel (Diamond Tooth Gertie to the miners) took me aside.

"Kitty, I'm worried about you. You're spoiling that man, and I'm afraid he's not good for you."

It was a brave thing for her to do, but of course I thought she was being too protective and did not thank her for her concern. When I was middle-aged and broke and she was married to the Yukon's most successful lawyer, I wished dearly I had paid her more heed, but at the time I was hopelessly in love. She could have shown me where it was written in the Bible that Alexander Pantages would do me wrong and I still would have found a way to ignore her. She called him "the patent leather kid" because the hair oil he used made his black hair shine like dance shoes—at the time it irritated me, but remembering it later brought me some comfort.

The truth was that Alex was not quite as attentive after we moved in together, and we ran into hardship after hardship. Fire gutted our theatre, not once, but three times. Each time we rebuilt, each time with me handing more of my nest egg over to Alex to manage the reconstruction.

Then, disastrously, I fell pregnant. We hadn't talked about what would happen if I became with child, but honestly, I thought we both assumed it would happen sooner or later. I loved our life in the theatre, and the idea of hiring someone to care for little Alex and continuing on with our plans made me happy. Surely Alexander would love me even more when I gave him a son—surely the boredom with which I sometimes caught him looking at me would disappear when I was the mother of his heir.

CHAPTER TEN

Canadian Creek was good to us, but we had good and bad years there. Good years, bad years, and one truly terrible year.

That summer, we watched on our satellite TV as gold prices continued their downward spiral. Each day my stomach turned as we watched the commodity market reports.

We had gold, lots of it. But it was worth so little, while the costs of diesel, wages and equipment payments stayed the same or went up.

I didn't do well with late payments and phone calls from creditors. It felt as if we'd been cursed—in addition to the fact that the world seemed to have decided it no longer needed gold, we had one equipment breakdown after another, with repair costs in the thousands of dollars each time.

Then the motor exploded in the D10N bulldozer, our largest piece of equipment, setting us back some eighty-thousand dollars. It pushed us over the edge.

One by one, our payments fell behind. The stress was too much for me, and I often lashed out at Dean. I trusted him to know what to do to fix the situation we were in, and it felt like he was deliberately letting me suffer.

Paying the employees was always first on my list, then fuel and food. Then equipment payments. Everything was leased;

we didn't own any of it, and the fees were tens of thousands of dollars a month.

Soon we were months behind, and unable to catch up. I sent what I could, but the amounts owing were so large they snowballed. We were up to our necks in defaulted loan payments.

If you totalled everything we had to pay out each month, including the mortgage for our home in BC, our lease payments for vehicles, and insurance for it all (equipment, life, house, vehicles etc.) it topped sixty thousand dollars each month. Not including surprise breakdowns. The pressure on us both was intense.

As the price of gold had fallen, we'd risen to the challenge. We got a head start on the season by arriving in camp as early as we could, living for the first few weeks without running water. I had learned to fill all the essential roles at camp, so if we couldn't afford help, I put that hat on top of whatever others I was wearing at the time. I was the supply manager, human resources manager, janitor, equipment operator, bookkeeper, parts person, expediter, cook and wife. I arranged for everything that was brought into camp, whether it was by barge, plane or helicopter. I hired machine operators and cooks to replace those who didn't last the season, often quitting with little or no notice, deciding to leave on a plane that had flown in with supplies.

I would fill their position myself while I placed ads in employment centres and newspapers, along with all the other things that needed my attention.

I honestly enjoyed doing a little bit of everything. Running equipment for twelve hours a day was deadly dull, and brutal on the body. I'd started to get a lot of migraines and chronic pain. Later I'd be diagnosed with fibromyalgia; at the time, I tried to manage with Tylenol or Ibuprofen and rest.

The rest was critical, but Dean wasn't sympathetic. I was to work the same long hours everyone else did. And I did. Most days started in the kitchen at six o'clock and ended well after midnight.

Still in my thirties, I was able to push through, but it took a toll. I began having anxiety attacks. It was as if my body was furiously trying to get my attention. I became obsessed with the idea that whatever issue I was having at the time was the beginning of a major medical emergency, and I would panic, knowing that I couldn't just drive to an emergency room or even to a doctor.

It got so bad that sometimes the only way for me to go on was to call for an airplane or helicopter so I could get medical care in town. It was a very expensive solution, and Dean was always furious.

The doctor would reassure me, prescribe a cream or a pill, and send me on my way. I always felt better after and could then go back to work.

The truth was that I couldn't handle the stresses of our financial situation, living in a remote camp, and our increasingly unhappy marriage. I don't know if anyone could, really. I didn't let myself notice that my panic disappeared not when the doctor told me I'd be okay, but as soon as I landed in town.

These attacks became more frequent and even more terrifying. I still loved mining, but living so remotely was wearing on me.

Dean and I began to fight a lot, mostly about money. As the price of gold fell, our relationship went with it. We got into arguments that escalated into screaming matches. I panicked and he raged.

One day, despite the grizzly phobia I'd developed, I hiked

down to the work site. He wouldn't answer me on the radio, and I needed him to change the propane tank that was connected to our stove so I could make dinner for the crew. The spare was a few miles away and I had no way of picking it up.

I could make out two of the guys sitting at the top of the plant beside Dean, who was bent over, shovelling dirt by hand and throwing it over the edge. The plant was disabled, and it looked like Dean was doing all the manual labour while the guys looked on. He looked angry and frustrated, but I knew everyone would be angry and frustrated if there was no dinner for the crew.

I yelled up that I needed Dean's help at camp. He didn't respond, so I assumed he couldn't hear me and yelled again a bit louder. There was no response from him, but one of the other guys looked my way, and I realized Dean was ignoring me.

I lost it—"it" being my sense of perspective and my temper.

"Dean, will you please get the fuck off of the plant and come talk to me!?"

He threw down his shovel, leapt down the long ladder to the deck and jumped off the four-foot-high skids. In what seemed like one fluid movement, he and I stood face to face.

I still didn't expect him to say the things he did.

"How dare you embarrass me in front of the crew?"

Sure. I'd apologize for that.

"You stupid, fucking ****!!"

Um, that wasn't okay. It was our crew—they had to respect me too. But when I pushed back verbally, he grabbed my arm and pulled me away from the cut. As he pushed me in front of him toward the house, I began to cry, frightened, and told him I was sorry for yelling at him.

He shoved me hard through the door, and when I tried to

close it on him, he knocked it open, the force throwing me backward. I tried to scramble to my feet, but he grabbed my hair and dragged me across the kitchen floor like a caveman. It felt as though my hair was being ripped from its roots. I was screaming in pain and fear, but I knew there was no one near enough to hear me.

I finally managed to break free and run away, but he caught up with me on the gravel trail that led to our cabin. I fell as he grabbed me, and scrambled on to my hands and knees to get away, the coarse gravel tearing the skin from my knees.

I finally managed to get to my feet and ran until I made it back to our cabin. As if it came from somewhere outside me, I became aware of a keening, sobbing cry, the sound of a frightened animal. It streamed from me as if I had nothing to do with it at all. I was terrified, and kept apologizing as he followed me inside. He just kept calling me awful names and telling me to get the fuck out, to go home.

I reached for the satellite phone to call a pilot, but Dean leaped over the desk and ripped it out of my hands. He yanked the plug out from the wall and grabbed the case that held the telephone. He took the whole thing with him as he stormed out, yelling back at me that I "wasn't fucking going anywhere."

I wanted to be home so badly. Anywhere but there.

Dean and I had always fought; we were both stubborn, independent people. I didn't like him telling me what to do and the same went for him. Until that day, though, I had trusted him. Now I was scared to death, but there was no way for me to get out and nowhere for me to go.

I cried helplessly, with fear, frustration and grief in equal parts leaking down my cheeks.

About twenty minutes had passed when I heard a four-wheeler driving up the road. I was relieved to see that it was Shawn.

I stumbled out the front door and yelled out to him. My face was still streaked with tears and my knees oozed blood. I blurted out what had happened and begged him to find Dean and get the telephone so I could call for a plane.

I was embarrassed and humiliated, but I had no one else to turn to. Shawn was quiet as he listened. Finally, he said, "I'll try," and jumped back on his ATV.

He drove off and I didn't see him again that day. When they came in, the crew figured out quickly that they had to scramble up something for themselves that night, as their dinner casserole sat uncooked in the cold oven.

Later that night Dean walked in, ignored me and headed straight to the bedroom to sleep.

The next morning, I quietly snuck out and headed over to the kitchen, first cleaning the dirty dishes that the crew had left on the table from the night before. Dean arrived shortly after; we didn't speak. I was stiff and in searing pain.

The guys started to show up for breakfast one by one, chatting among themselves. Shawn wouldn't even look at me.

Until then, our crew had felt like family to me. But maybe that's the way some families are, too. No one ever asked if I was okay.

Dean was never that physically brutal with me again. He didn't have to be. He'd killed my spirit and my self-respect. I spent the rest of our years together trying not to provoke him, because I wasn't sure I could live through another day like that one.

It was me who felt guilt, not him. I was to blame; I should never have yelled at him.

It was only much later that I began to see that I was part of a pattern. Dean blamed his father for ruining his life by taking him out of school at a young age. He had no respect for his mother and said horrible things about her. Our crew was to blame for everything that went wrong at work.

Yet I defended him to the end. I would have done anything for him, anything he needed me to do. He'd made me believe that he would do the same for me and even when he proved it wasn't true, I kept waiting for the man who'd made those promises. It felt as if this person, this Dean, had betrayed us both, and I could only wait and hope for the real Dean to reappear.

Over time, I'd let my many friends drift away. Dean made me feel that everyone else I was close to was "stupid" and not worthy of our time.

I thought he was everything I needed. And Shawn was our best friend and partner.

After Shawn chose not to help me in my worst moment, I never asked for help from anyone ever again.

By the end of that season, we knew we were in deep trouble with the equipment dealer. Whenever our mail was brought in with our supply order, it was full of envelopes with "Final Notice!" stamped in red across the front. The threatening phone calls never stopped; we just stopped answering.

Dean convinced us that we'd catch up next season and everything would be fine.

Snow began to fall, but we stayed in camp and worked tirelessly, trying to pull out enough gold to survive the winter back home and fund next year's start-up costs.

Only Dean, Shawn and I were left in camp, struggling

through snow, ice and fatigue. Later we'd find out we were the only miners still in camp in the entire Yukon.

Freezing water was our nemesis. We wrapped our water lines in heat tape and put space heaters underneath the floors, desperately trying to keep our kitchen operating.

The creek was low at this time of year and many mornings we'd wake to find it frozen over. Without a running creek, we couldn't sluice. It was inevitable—lack of water would bring our season to an end soon. But we refused to give up.

We were all beyond exhausted; you could see it. Shawn had lost a fair amount of weight; Dean had huge bags under his eyes and his hair was thinning a lot.

In our last few weeks in camp, it was up to me to pack up. It was a big job, cleaning and putting everything away for the winter. Everything was packed into boxes that were then put inside large black garbage bags, ready for next season. Our bedding, pillows and mattresses needed to be protected from the animals that would surely make their way inside over the winter.

Occasionally we'd come back in the spring to find our cabins destroyed by a bear that had made its way down the hill after waking from hibernation. They woke up starving, and would find a way in no matter how prepared we thought we were, breaking windows or using their claws to rip off the plywood we nailed over the windows and doors. One year we had to deal with an angry wolverine that had somehow found its way inside, a surly creature with long claws and ferocious-looking teeth.

Dean and Shawn appreciated it when I brought hot soup and warm homemade buns down to them on the mine site. Food was the highlight of the day for them—other than that, it was just relentless, backbreaking work.

Just as I was packing up the lunch box one day, I heard a helicopter in the distance. Mystified, I ran out onto the deck, the screen door slamming behind me. Straining to see who it was, I recognized the distinct colour of the Fireweed chopper. It was flying low down the valley towards the sluice plant.

It was odd for a helicopter to fly into camp without us knowing who it was in advance. Claims inspectors dropped in once a month to check on our operation and ensure we were doing everything according to mining regulations, but they'd been in just a few weeks earlier.

Their visits were almost always a surprise, but why would they be back so soon? I had a bad feeling.

I left the lunches on the counter and grabbed my jacket and boots. Jumping onto my ATV, I drove as fast as I could towards the plant. When I arrived, the helicopter had already landed.

There were four men talking to Dean. I didn't recognize any of them except for the pilot. I could tell something was very wrong by the look on Dean's face.

His eyes were laser-focused on the man talking to him, his head slightly cocked to one side. He rested his chin on his thumb, his pointer finger tapping the outer corner of his mouth, which curved upward in a grin that looked anything but friendly. It was Dean's signature "I'm going to fuck you up" look. We all knew that look. It was extremely intimidating.

I walked slowly towards them, catching parts of the conversation as I got closer. They were bailiffs, sent by the machinery company we owed so much money.

I felt sick. We hadn't imagined that someone would come in at this time of the year. We were sure we had until next spring, when we'd be able to start producing again and catch up with our payments.

The bailiffs were big, menacing guys, and they were there to seize our equipment.

It was an abrupt end to our season. We barely had enough money to make our payments at home. I was devastated, and Dean was ready to kill. He refused to hand over the keys, but it didn't matter. They'd brought their own.

We learned later on that these guys had to walk the equipment out of camp, overland on a winter road. It must have taken them days. I didn't envy them at all.

Back home, my doctor told me I had ulcers; some of the worst panic attacks of my life had happened during that long winter. I was positive we wouldn't be back mining again.

But Dean was a fighter—he never gave up. He heard through the grapevine that our equipment was going up for auction and found an investor who wanted to be a silent partner. We located another mine site—still remote, but with a road that made it possible to drive to Dawson City!

Dean was excited. It felt like a fresh new beginning. The interminable stress and isolation were behind us; this new operation would undoubtedly turn things around.

I couldn't wait for spring.

We laughed about the hired goons who'd worked so hard to take our equipment and what went through their minds when they realized it was us that bought the equipment at auction, for half the amount we owed and would otherwise have paid.

I'd have cause to cry about that laughter later.

CHAPTER ELEVEN

We'd leased some promising claims from a couple of old-time mining partners, one from Alberta and the other from Arizona. They gave us a big sales pitch about how rich their creek was and how easy it would be to mine with our equipment.

Every claim owner in the Yukon will tell you how rich their ground is when they want to sell it; depending on who they're talking to, the same claim can be "shit." Lots of smoke and mirrors. But we made a deal and packed up Canadian Creek, leaving our beautiful log house and cabins to the bears and the wind.

Dean and I flew into the new claims on Matson Creek by helicopter late in the fall. We were excited to see our new camp but also a bit nervous about what shape we'd find things in.

We decided to touch down first at the airstrip to get a look at its condition. A lifeless orange windsock hung high on a metal pole, tattered by many years of unforgiving winter storms. At the end of the strip was an old shed with a large rack of moose antlers nailed above the door. It was typical for the North, but the display of dead animal parts never sat right with me, and I took them down soon after our arrival.

Our lease included some old equipment and a battered pickup truck that served as transportation around camp.

I had heard interesting rumours about the man who had originally staked this creek back in the early 1900s. Many men had stayed and continued to search for gold after the rush had fizzled out, but the claims close to town were taken or mined out early. Newer prospectors had to resort to mining the more remote creeks, like this one.

John Matson was said to be a quiet, small man, born in Norway. In 1896, he became a US citizen. There is no record of him becoming a Canadian citizen, even though he would live here most of his life.

John spoke limited English when he arrived in the Yukon after making the long trek from California. He staked his claim on December 18, 1911, and the creek was later named after him. He would mine here until 1946, when he died at age eighty-two.

The RCMP were satisfied that his death was "by natural causes," but not everyone was convinced. Whatever had happened, the gold he'd mined since his last trek to town was never found, and many people have since made it their business to search his cabin and land to find it.

I found these stories intriguing, especially now that we were on his claim. Stepping down onto the dirt runway, I pulled my jacket tightly around me and wiggled my toes inside the fur-lined mukluks that kept my feet toasty whatever the weather.

The valley and hillsides that surrounded us were eerily quiet, the view vast and beautiful. The early morning fog lay well below the airstrip, close to the valley floor.

Up here the air was crisp. I instinctively closed my eyes and took a deep, full breath. As I exhaled, I realized that I felt completely at home in the North. It had been a terrible time, but it was behind us. Everything would be better now.

I noticed a large rock outcropping high on a snow-covered hill, about a quarter-mile from where we stood.

"If I were John Matson, that rock face is where I would hide my gold," I said to Dean.

He laughed out loud. "Why?"

"You would always see those rocks, whether it was winter, spring, summer or fall."

"If it was that easy, I think someone would have found it by now," he said. "People have been looking for years. Decades."

I agreed. But I also wanted to climb that hill as soon as possible. I somehow knew I would find something important there.

Dean and the pilot walked the airstrip while I cautiously found a place to pee. Bears would be scouring the hills in search of food before going into hibernation for the winter, and I didn't want to be it.

After a few more minutes scouting the airstrip and investigating the contents of the shed, we took a quick look at the abandoned vehicles and diesel barrels that were left scattered about.

We climbed back onboard the chopper and flew a few minutes down the valley, landing again near the camp bunkhouses.

It wasn't anything at all like the beautiful log home and cabins we were leaving behind, but I liked it. There were six trailers, each with its own bedroom, kitchen and bathroom. We would convert the largest one into the main kitchen for breakfast and dinners.

The camp was high above the mine site, and I loved the view. I could see for miles up and down the valley from our window. I marvelled at how wide open it all was, and so different than Canadian Creek. I couldn't wait to get started.

There was still a tremendous amount of work ahead of us, bringing all of our equipment and supplies in. We were able to haul in a limited amount by air, but almost everything had to be brought over many miles of treacherous road.

Dean didn't know much about the road leading into camp from Sixtymile, the intersection with the nearest real road, but what he had heard was all bad. According to the people who had traveled it, it was more mountain goat trail than road.

I only heard "road," though—one I could potentially drive into town on. Just the word made me feel less isolated, claustrophobic and unsafe.

After spending a few hours inspecting our new site, we flew the fifty minutes or so back to Dawson City for a few nights' rest. We were gearing up for another adventure, so we needed to have a couple of days of quality sleep and time to gather supplies.

We stayed at our favourite hotel, Bombay Peggy's, which was originally run as a brothel and bootlegger. In 1997, it was bought by two local women who transformed it with lavishly decorated rooms and a sumptuous bar tucked away on the main floor.

Each room was known by its decor, including the Gold Room, the Purple Room and the ever-popular Lipstick Room. The furnishings are reminiscent of the Klondike era, with claw-foot tubs, weathered oriental carpets, antique furniture and fluffy down duvets.

Our regular room was on the second floor, overlooking the hustle and bustle of Princess Street, called the "Sweet." It was huge, and charming, and I felt so spoiled whenever we stayed there. It reminded me of everything I had read about Kate's suite at the Grand, and I felt almost as if I could knock on her door and invite her over for a drink. I spent an embarrassing amount of time talking to her in my mind, telling her about everything I'd been through and how much her strength and story inspired me to continue on. She never said much back, but I could almost hear her laughter, and I always felt her friendship.

In addition to feeling like we were living in the gold rush at Peggy's, I loved that each morning started with freshly baked, warm croissants and homemade jam, each one wrapped lovingly in printed napkins and hung from our door handle. It was like the little hotel fairies knew exactly when we were awake.

After coffee, a long, hot shower and delectable croissants, Dean and I checked out on our third day. We were on our way to Sixtymile, about ninety minutes from Dawson City by land.

We crossed the Yukon River by ferry, a ten-minute ride, and then drove the rest of the way on a rough gravel road, wittily named the "Top of the World Highway." This so-called highway was brutal, filled with potholes, but it really felt like the top of the world, looking down on sweeping views that seemed endless.

About an hour into the trip, we turned off of the "highway" and started down into the Sixtymile valley, where the road ran past numerous mining operations. Many were operated by miners I admired, mining families that had been in the area for years and had done very well for themselves.

Not too far down into the valley, a large and dirty pickup truck slowed to a stop. The driver rolled his window down, the universal signal he wanted to talk.

Dean recognized him. Stan Schneider was well known in the mining world and he and his wife owned a successful Dawson jewelry store that she ran while he was out on their claims.

Stan also owned his own airplane. It was similar to the other bush planes in the area, except that, according to what Dean had heard, his had lots of power.

Stan mentioned that the river up ahead was impossible to cross because the water was so high. Listening to him, I was concerned, but I didn't say anything. I was pretty confident that Dean would figure out a way to cross safely.

Stan said he was also worried about the road into Matson Creek. "No disrespect, folks, but you're crazy to even try it at this time of the year."

We chatted a bit longer and Stan decided to turn around and follow us back to the Sixtymile River to watch us try to cross. Great. I liked Stan, but I did not need an audience.

As we neared the river, we could see that the water was so high that waves crashed over the banks. On the other side, a pickup truck with a camper was parked, trapped by the high water. A few people were milling around on our side of the river, friends of his who were trying to help.

Our excavator sat off to the side of the road, along with a barrel of diesel and a fuel pump. We'd had it brought here a week or so earlier. My job was "walking" the excavator overland to our camp while Dean drove the truck in. Then we would fly back and meet up with our crew to bring everything else into camp together. A helicopter would pick us up the next afternoon at Matson Creek.

The plan was to fix the rocky road along the way, making it possible to haul in the rest of our equipment.

Slowly, more people started to show up, local miners coming to watch the idiots attempting to cross the swollen river.

Dean told me to start the excavator and load the barrel of diesel and pump into the box of the truck. The plan was Dean's, and although I was committed to doing the best I could, the truth is I was absolutely terrified. To make things worse, our audience had grown. I kept telling myself I could do it—I was brave! I was fierce! I would show everyone that I had no fear. I was Klondike Kate. Like her, I wouldn't let anything get in my way. But now I thought I knew how she had felt—scared to death!

Dean started the pickup truck and slowly entered the raging water. Over the radio, he gave me instructions, explaining that I had to walk the excavator into the river alongside the truck to keep it from washing away in the current.

Under no circumstances was I to move slower or faster than the truck, or it and Dean would be swept away.

As we neared the middle of the river, the bottom below me dropped away. The metal tracks of the excavator tipped forward and I instinctively lowered the bucket to stabilize the machine. I looked over at Dean and saw water flowing up and over the hood of his truck. The cab was filling with the icy water, and the truck was now floating, no longer drivable. By some miracle I was able to keep him by my side, the pickup's passenger door scraping against the metal tracks of the excavator. My hands dripping with sweat, I prayed out loud that we would somehow make it to the other side. At that moment, we moved into more shallow water; Dean's tires touched the bottom and grabbed hold. He was able to drive out on his own and I made it to the other side a few seconds later. The inside of the excavator was flooded and we were both wet, but I was so relieved we'd made it in one piece!

The fellow who had been standing in his camper door was now running towards us, flabbergasted. Everyone on the other side of the river was clapping and cheering, amazed that we had actually pulled it off.

I felt proud of myself and Dean yelled out, "Good job!!"

I could not believe what we had just managed to do. We learned that the man in the camper had been waiting for the river to recede for about a week. He said he had plenty of food to wait it out, so we chatted for a few minutes longer and then said our goodbyes, waving to Stan and the others watching us from across the river.

I naively thought we'd made it through the most harrowing part of the trip. I should have known better.

The next few hours were spent fixing parts of the road that had been pretty much destroyed by the heavy rains and runoffs over the last few years. As the day wore on, we moved higher and higher up the mountainside. The excavator's top speed was about four miles per hour on a good road, so it was an extremely slow, rough ride, but I felt safer than in the truck.

My anxiety increased as we climbed. The road was now so narrow that one track of the excavator was right on the edge of the bank, and the bank was soft. We had climbed so high that if it gave way, I would plunge with the excavator to the valley below; the chances of living through that were extremely slim. The clouds were thick all around us and it was hard to see even a few feet ahead. To make things worse, snow had fallen up here and the metal tracks often slid suddenly down towards the edge. There were a couple of times I had to grab hold of the icy ground with the digging bucket to stop the excavator from sliding off. When I did, the rocks and dirt tumbling down to the valley floor carried my stomach with them, vertigo rising in me until I had to stop and rest my forehead on my lap to let the swirling world still again. It was impossible, impassible, and yet there was no way out.

I kept telling Dean how scared I was over the radio, telling him we had to go back, and he grew more and more frustrated with me.

Finally, he drove out of radio range, and I could no longer

see or talk to him. Tears ran steadily down my face and I didn't even bother to wipe them away. I had reached what felt like peak stress and I was completely alone. The person I loved most in the world was fine with the danger I was in, and felt I should be okay with it too. I felt abandoned and was sure he'd left me to die alone on this awful road. I envisioned Dean sliding over the edge himself. I thought of my family at home, unaware that we were making this foolish, hazardous trip.

I was well aware that I was having a major panic attack and kept trying to calm myself, but it is not easy to do when you're sliding from one near-death experience to the next.

Yet I managed to keep moving forward—it felt like there was nothing else to do. Hours later, the clouds lifted slightly and I could once again see the road ahead of me as it wound its way up to the top of the mountain. It grew even narrower, the excavator crashing down hard on boulders that protruded from massive holes. By then, my anxiety and fear had become fury at Dean.

I heard an engine.

He had finally come back to look for me!

I stopped the machine and opened the window to listen. The fog lay thick around me but there was a small break in the clouds above. I couldn't figure out where the noise was coming from. Then, like something out of a movie, a plane dropped down through the opening in the clouds and flew beside me, dipping one wing. I could see Stan in the pilot's seat; he was so close I could see his big smile. I waved frantically at him and he gave me the thumbs up sign. I turned my thumbs up to him, and then he was gone, once again disappearing into the clouds. I learned later that he was so worried about us that he wanted to check to make sure nothing had happened.

I wasn't ready to see him go. "Come back!" I yelled. But Stan was already gone, the sound of his plane fading away.

I'd given up my single chance for rescue. I couldn't stop now—I refused to fail.

Many harrowing hours later, I made it to the top of the mountain. I rounded a corner and saw Dean in the pickup on the road ahead.

I was ecstatic to see him.

I was also so livid that I yelled at him as soon as I could get out of my seat, telling him that he was a horrible husband.

Of course, that didn't sit well with him, and as usual, he responded with words of his own, carefully crafted to make me feel awful about myself.

We soon agreed on one thing—it was all my fault.

Look at us—we were fine! Why was I always making nothing into something?

Over our years in the Yukon, I didn't heal from these experiences. It was almost as if being belittled for fearing for our lives made it impossible to move on. Over time, I became fearful of everything, locked into a constant state of flight-or-fight.

It took twenty-two hours to reach Matson Creek after crossing the river. Those hours are seared into my bones.

CHAPTER TWELVE

Dean and I met Grant, the investor who helped to buy our equipment back from auction, at the gold buyer's office in Dawson City. We thought it was an accidental meeting, but learned later that Grant was in Dawson City to be introduced to us.

He seemed like a nice guy and we talked for hours. A Canadian mining industry investor, he had offices in Calgary and lived in Honduras. He told us about his mining and smelting operations there and said he was looking for a Canadian mining partner. It was all very interesting, but we were so focused on the challenges with our Canadian operations at the time that it seemed out of the question.

Grant insisted that we at least come to take a look and, if nothing else, make a holiday of it. We decided to fly down after our season in the Yukon. We had no idea that our circumstances would be so dire by then, and that a partner would be the perfect (and perhaps only) solution to our predicament.

I was thrilled to go. I loved to travel and jumped at pretty much any chance to explore somewhere new. Dean and I had visited many countries by then, but Central America would be a first for us both. I conducted my usual pre-trip research and learned that Honduras was not one of the safest places to visit, but flying down in mid-January still seemed like a great way to escape winter.

There were no direct flights from Vancouver, so we flew to Los Angeles, on to Houston for an overnight layover, and then to Guatemala, before finally landing in Tegucigalpa, the capital city.

Our departure from Vancouver was memorable. Dean walked ahead of me towards the airport screening area, and when we reached the scanning conveyor, he emptied his pockets and put his boarding pass, wallet and loose change into a plastic bin. Then he reached down and, using both hands, hoisted his black leather briefcase onto the conveyor belt. The solid thud made its weight obvious.

One of the officers motioned Dean through the metal detector and I watched as his briefcase slowly entered the X-ray machine. I loaded the large suitcase we shared onto the scanner, along with my purse. The conveyor belt jerked to a stop, and one of the security guards motioned another officer over to look at the images of Dean's briefcase. Four more officers hurried over, one of them firing questions at Dean, another quietly asking me if we were together. When I said yes, we were both taken to a small room beside the security operations, leaving our fellow travellers in line all looking a bit concerned.

Once inside, the security officers asked more rapid-fire questions and told Dean to open the black case. As he lifted the top, they all backed up against the wall. I'm sure they suspected a bomb, since the X-ray showed a large, dense mass filling the inside of the case.

Dean loved this game. He smirked the whole time, anticipating the reaction he was about to get.

"It's raw gold," he said, removing the lid so they could see inside.

"Are you joking? That's gold?" one asked. They all leaned in, looking a lot more relaxed than they had a moment before.

We poured some of the flaky, shimmery metal onto a plate so they could get a better look. They started taking pictures and chattering, fascinated.

Gold fever. It takes hold of you just like that.

Most people think it's illegal to carry more than ten thousand dollars' worth of gold over national borders, but you can carry as much raw, unrefined gold as you want, as long as you report it to officials upon boarding. On international flights, we only had to provide proof that we'd paid any tax or royalties owed to the originating country and that we were the rightful owner. We were not required to pay tax on raw placer gold until it was smelted and sold, and miners in the Yukon paid a ridiculously low royalty rate to the government, around thirty-eight cents per ounce. (At that time, on $100,000 worth of gold, we owed the territory $160.)

This case was destined for Grant, who had asked to buy it, supposedly to test the purity of the gold we mined in the Yukon.

I wondered what the rest of the passengers thought when we reappeared from the security office, the five officers with us now laughing, talking and eager to shake our hands before waving us through.

Above Guatemala City the following day, the pilot circled the airport, banking so hard that I had to hold my seat to keep from sliding onto the window. As we began to level out, I could see that we were flying extremely low, directly over a major highway. Traffic lights flashed red at either end of the road, stopping all vehicles. Our commercial jet fell quickly, skimming the highway, and we hit the runway hard. The wheels screeched, smoke billowed into the air, and I braced myself with both hands against the seat in front of me to avoid being flung into it. As we came to a stop, everyone on the plane unexpectedly erupted, applauding and cheering. The person next to me said that passengers always clapped when a pilot made a successful landing here—we'd just landed at the second most extreme commercial airport in the world. The approach is so difficult that pilots are required to have special training.

We made our way into the one-room airport and lined up to wait our turn in security. I worried that it would be difficult explaining the gold we carried to the Spanish-speaking police and was relieved when they just waved us through. We soon boarded a smaller plane and landed uneventfully in Tegucigalpa.

I was shocked to see that the ramp leading to the front doors of the Tegucigalpa airport was enclosed by a ten-foot-high wire fence. People crowded against it, some crawling up the wire and yelling. It was frightening.

At the end of the ramp a man held a cardboard sign with our names scribbled in black felt marker. He explained that he'd been sent to drive us to Grant's home, and led us to a waiting sedan, its windows completely blacked out.

As we drove, I saw hundreds of people walking tiredly beside the dirty roads. There were women in long, tattered skirts and sandals, some carrying small children. Men rode rusted bicycles with teenagers perched behind them. The road was busy with battered buses and cars. The many pickup trucks were often loaded to overflowing with fruit, and on top of the fruit, people sat holding on for dear life. I was sure someone was going to fall and be killed right in front of us.

Honduras' population was around 6.6 million people at that time, and 800,000 of them lived in Tegucigalpa. More than half the population lived in extreme, life-and-death poverty. It is bordered by Guatemala, Nicaragua, and El Salvador, all countries that brought news images of machine guns, kidnapping and civil war to mind.

We reached an affluent area, with fifteen-foot cement walls surrounding the hidden homes. Each wall was topped with coiled razor-sharp wire and jagged chunks of glass.

As we pulled up to a gate, a uniformed man carrying an automatic gun came towards our vehicle. He spoke to our driver in Spanish and the driver rolled down the car's windows. The guard circled us, inspecting everything inside and out before waving us on.

"Welcome to Mr. Grant's Casa Grande," the driver said in heavily Spanish-inflected English as huge wrought iron gates opened to allow us to enter the courtyard. A sprawling rancher was tucked inside under a canopy of flowers, its walls painted a sunny mustard yellow. The gardens were lush, the air sweet with the scents of jasmine and magnolia. I was instantly enchanted.

The driver opened our doors and I stepped out onto the cobblestone driveway.

Grant appeared and shook Dean's hand, hard, before giving me a big bear hug and lifting my feet off the ground.

Grant was a big man, around six-foot-four, large-boned, with hands as large as baseball gloves. I guessed him to be around sixty, and his cloud-white hair and piercing, ice-blue eyes gave him a distinctive appearance.

He told the driver to take our luggage to our room and then gave us a tour of the house, where the lavish artwork seemed to be of museum quality. In the middle of his sitting room was a huge, elaborately carved wooden chair, like something King Henry himself would have sat on.

It seemed our new friend was impressively wealthy—and a bit eccentric.

We followed him into his office and someone on his staff brought in a tray of cold drinks. The conversation turned to the many signed Canadian and American hockey jerseys that hung on the walls of his large office. Grant said he had once played for the NHL but had to retire because of an injury.

He treated us like royalty and insisted on paying for everything, including our flights. I was delighted to learn that he even had a personal masseuse on staff that he invited us to call on whenever we wanted.

That first night we enjoyed a sumptuous dinner created by Grant's personal chef, and the next day he drove us to see the gold refinery, another part of his Honduran operation. Dean and I were impressed.

We decided to take him up on his offer and work in Honduras during our off season. Everything seemed to fall into place quickly and we extended our trip to buy a bulldozer and the other equipment we'd need, all of it funded by Grant.

We flew home, planning to return once we had hired a few key people and shipped in the supplies we couldn't buy there. Our deal with Grant included enough money to buy back our equipment in the Yukon—we would mine in Canada for the four or five warmest months of the year and in Honduras for the rest.

We were thrilled—it seemed like a win for everyone involved and our work and potential for wealth had just gone international.

Because there wasn't much I could do until the mine was in operation, Dean returned to Honduras without me, bringing two men who would help him hire and train the rest of the workers locally. The mine site was about four hours from Tegucigalpa by road, in the dusty desert province of Olancho.

My first trip back to Honduras two months later was really just a visit to check out the new operations and the camp. I was full of enthusiasm but not sure what to expect.

At the airport, I was picked up by Wes, an American who had worked in the personal security industry there for many years. Grant had hired him as part of our security team. We talked a lot while driving to the site and I learned that he would be my personal bodyguard for the entire trip.

I was shocked to learn that I needed security. Wes had protected a couple of Americans before meeting Grant, and he quickly opened my eyes to the dangers there, including the widespread practice of kidnapping for ransom.

After an uneventful drive on the main highway, we turned off and travelled down a dusty, winding road, at one point crossing a wooden bridge so narrow and dilapidated that I wondered how the crew had brought equipment over without destroying it.

We passed many small farms with an underfed cow or two in the fields, their ribs and hip bones protruding.

We rounded the last corner and I saw the camp, an old farmhouse we'd rented from some locals. Dean was waiting for me at the front doors. I was so happy to see him—we had been apart for over two months, after many years of being together almost twenty-four hours a day.

He gave me a tour of the property and introduced me to the camp horse and cat, resting together in the shade of an impressively large mahogany tree.

Our friend Rick came over to give me a big hug and ask about my trip. Rick was a mining engineer from Whitehorse, a skilled sluice plant expert who had helped us out many times over the years in Canada.

I was curious to see the kitchen, so they led me up to the house.

On the way, I noticed two pretty young women standing on the covered porch. One had her arm around the other, as if she were consoling her. They spoke quietly in Spanish. I felt only curiosity until I noticed that the one being consoled was watching me closely, her expression fierce. I couldn't help notice the large gun on her belt.

I asked Dean who they were, and he explained that the one with the gun was ex-police from Tegucigalpa, one of the camp's security team. The other was the cook and housekeeper.

I told myself that the ex-police woman was watching me with suspicion because I was new to the camp, but something felt wrong.

Later, we all went to the nearest village, which had a population of about a hundred people and homes of mud and straw, with pieces of rusty old metal for roofs.

The residents seemed happy when we arrived, and the kids all came running because the crew always passed out candy when they visited.

The security team was with us every minute of the day, wearing flak jackets and carrying machine guns. Despite this, or perhaps because of it, I never felt safe.

As the sun fell lower in the sky, Wes interrupted the non-stop conversation to say it was time for us to head back to the city. The camp had few amenities and I was almost as afraid of the scorpions scurrying across the dirt floors of the bedrooms as I was of grizzlies. Dean and I had decided I would stay in Tegucigalpa at a casita we rented. I would pick up supplies for the mine site as needed, coming out to stay once in a while.

When Wes mentioned he was "a bit concerned" about the

four-hour drive back, I quickly said goodbye to Dean and the crew.

"I don't normally drive at all here after dark—it's too dangerous," Wes said.

That worried me, and I also couldn't keep my mind off the security woman who'd looked at me with such hostility.

The deserted highway was unsettling, too. No matter how much time I spent near the equator, I was always surprised by how suddenly the sun dropped below the horizon twelve hours after sunrise. Before long it was dark, only our car's lights cutting the inky blackness. Occasionally a few men would emerge onto the road from what seemed to be impenetrable darkness, often holding machetes. Each time I felt my stomach clench until we'd safely passed and the highway was once again deserted.

We were probably about halfway when Wes admitted that he was having terrible stomach pains, probably from something he had eaten, and needed to find a bathroom fast. He didn't want to stop, he said, but he had no choice. He wasn't going to make it back.

I trusted him, but I was also terrified.

He took a sharp turn off the highway and pulled into a dimly lit gas station, parking under the lamppost outside the entrance.

"I don't want to leave you here, Brandee, but if I don't go, I'm going to crap myself. I don't think either one of us wants that."

He smiled but his expression was still grim, and I could tell he was doing his best to lighten the mood. I really just wanted him to hurry. There was nothing I wanted less than to be alone in the middle of nowhere in this frightening country.

Wes took one of his pistols from his belt, opening the chamber to show me it was loaded, and showed me quickly how to use it.

Handing it to me, he said, "Do not unlock the doors, not for anyone. Use the gun if you need to."

He slammed the car door and ran into the dark. I reached over to check on the locks. My hands were shaking.

Only a few minutes passed before a small, beat-up black car pulled up beside me, Spanish-language rap blaring through its speakers. Two men emerged, laughing, one holding a bottle. The other had a gun sticking out from his jeans.

They both stopped and looked at our car, which stood out because it was at least ten times more valuable than any other vehicle we'd seen on the roads that day. They walked around it and one bent to the windows, cupping his eyes with his hands to try to see in. I felt as if my heart would explode, his face just inches from mine.

One tried the door handle and I cocked the gun. When the door didn't open, his partner tried the other doors, shaking the car as he did.

I held my breath, waiting for him to draw his gun and start shooting out the locks. I was trying to come to terms with the idea that I might have to kill someone to protect myself in this godforsaken place.

It seemed like forever, but it was probably only minutes before Wes reappeared. He shouted something at the two men in Spanish, and they walked quickly away.

As they disappeared into the dark, I reached over and unlocked Wes's door.

As soon as he locked it behind him again, I broke down, sobbing and shaking.

"Oh, God. I thought I was going to have to shoot those guys. Please don't ever do that again, Wes."

I could tell from his look that he felt that shooting two men was absolutely not the worst thing that could happen to me in Honduras alone after dark, but he said nothing.

I suddenly wanted to be back in Canada very badly. I had missed Dean and dreamt of rekindling our relationship in this exotic new place. Now I knew there was nothing here I wanted badly enough to die or kill for.

When we finally pulled into the compound where I would stay, I was limp with relief. The house was protected by high stone walls, a heavy iron gate and twenty-four-hour guards. Wes took me inside and introduced me to the cook who lived there, Ana. She was older, sixty-ish, and seemed very sweet. But she spoke no English.

Wes showed me to my room and handed me a sawed-off shotgun. "To keep under your bed, just in case."

Oh my God, I hate this place, I thought. This was not what I thought Honduras would be like—I'd pictured sleepy towns, beautiful beaches and friendly villagers. Instead, it felt more like a huge desert camp run by militia and cartels, and it was hard to tell which were which.

I stayed alone at the house for a few days, coming out of my room only to eat and shower. I tried to communicate with Ana, but we could only laugh uncomfortably at each other as she made me something to eat.

I had been so traumatized by my trip home from the mine that all I really wanted was to go home to peaceful Canada.

That night, there was a light knock on my bedroom door. I thought it was Ana bringing me the delicious fruit she often prepared as a late-night snack. I opened it casually.

Dean! Seeing him was such a joy that I forgot everything—

my fright, our fights, his rages—all our troubles of the last few years evaporated as I jumped into his arms and held him tightly to me.

I cried and kissed him over and over, asking what he was doing there. I had never been so happy to see anyone!

We sat on the edge of the bed and he told me that Wes had called to tell him about the gun incident. Dean thought it would be a nice surprise to come in and stay with me for a few days until I was settled in. I was so happy that he had.

The next morning, he said he wanted to introduce me to a friend he'd made after meeting him at the equipment dealership the friend owned. Eduardo was an American-born Honduran of French descent, about thirty, and extremely wealthy. His grandmother was the head of the family and they were well connected throughout the country.

I was in a much better mood and looked forward to meeting him. Dean seemed enamoured with him, which I found interesting—my husband was a hard man to impress.

A Mercedes with blacked-out windows was in the driveway waiting for us when we stepped out of the house. As we drove off, I noticed two or three other cars in front of us, a few more following behind.

I asked Dean what was going on.

"Your guess is as good as mine," he said.

As we drove slowly through the busy streets of Tegucigalpa, I started to notice that some motorcycles had now joined us in what seemed like a full-on motorcade. As we passed through the intersections, I could see that the motorcycles were police who shut down each intersection so we could drive through them without stopping.

Dean and I were in awe, watching as, one by one, each

intersection was blocked off to other traffic, people waving madly at us as we passed by.

"This is unbelievable! Why are they doing this for us?" I asked Dean.

He said he didn't know, but he told me later that Eduardo hadn't liked hearing that I was afraid in his country. "He wanted to make sure you felt safe here."

The whole day was unforgettably wonderful. We met Eduardo at a luxurious hotel where he took us for lunch. The food was delectable and so was his company. He was extremely intelligent, sophisticated, funny and handsome. Over the next few weeks, he took us for rides in his helicopter and on trips to Panama and Miami. He drove us to his sprawling, beautiful ranch to ride horses and meet his distinguished grandmother and gorgeous wife.

Eduardo seemed like the glamorous lead character in a movie, but as I got to know him, I realized that he was involved in crime. He also had a drug problem and considered it normal to cheat on his wife.

One day I overheard him tell Dean that, as long as you buy your wife expensive gifts like diamond bracelets and earrings or a Rolex, she would look the other way and be happy with whatever her husband wanted to do.

I didn't give it too much thought at the time, other than telling myself that it sounded like that was how wealthy men acted in his country, but I felt my affection and respect for Eduardo slipping away. I also felt sorry for his young and gorgeous wife, who seemed like a lovely person.

His words came back to me vividly on the plane as I headed back to Canada, however. I opened the gift that Dean had given me in the airport, telling me not to open it until I was in the air.

As I found myself looking through tears at a stunning, ruby-encrusted diamond necklace, I pictured the pretty security guard at the camp once again.

Dean spent five months in Honduras looking for gold. It turned out that Grant's desert gold mine was just desert. Later, he would be sentenced to twelve years for running a mining-themed Ponzi scheme that bilked Canadian investors of hundreds of millions of dollars, of which he served two. It's possible our briefcase of raw gold was used as part of the devastating seduction of what may have been as many as four thousand investors. Grant bought a throne for himself in his palatial estate in Honduras; many of the people who trusted him lost their pensions and ended up going back to work to make ends meet. But none of this came out until years later.

I never found out for sure if my fears about the beautiful security guard were true. After I talked to Dean and he denied it, citing my wild imagination and anxious nature as the source of any problem, I decided to put it out of my mind.

By then we were back in Canada together, and it was time to move on.

CHAPTER THIRTEEN

During our first few months at Matson Creek, I begged Dean to take a day off and hike with me to the rock outcropping. I couldn't stop thinking about what I might find there, and I couldn't go alone, because … grizzlies.

Dean finally agreed to go on the hike with me and we decided to set off right after breakfast the next day. I put together a picnic lunch and packed two handheld radios so we could contact someone from the crew if we needed help. I also packed a compass, extra clothing, and lots of water. I stuck a note on the fridge:

Don't forget lunch and a gun!

I was definitely overly prepared for the short hike, but my experiences in the woods had made me cautious.

It was the summer solstice, meaning that the sun was above the horizon for a full twenty-four hours. At about five in the morning, the sound of something moving outside our bedroom woke me up. I crawled over Dean, who slept the dead sleep of exhaustion, and pulled the blackout blind away from the window to have a look. Just a few yards away was a massive, almost white grizzly. I could see her unmistakable shoulder hump; I guessed she weighed more than a thousand pounds. She was so close I could see her black eyes and her short, rounded ears. Just as shocking was the size of the cubs on either side of her.

I shook Dean hard. "There are bears outside!"

As the words came out of my mouth, there was a loud crash at the other end of our trailer. Dean shot up and out of bed. As he ran out of the room, the trailer started to shake violently, as if someone was ramming it over and over with a truck.

"Get the fucking gun, get the gun, get the gun!" he yelled.

I could hear glass shattering as I grabbed the rifle from the closet. I ran right into Dean as I flew out of the bedroom, and he yanked the gun from my hand. Now we could hear wood splintering and metal tearing.

"Shoot it! Oh my God, shoot it!" I screamed, petrified. I couldn't understand why Dean wasn't firing. The bear was coming through the wall in our laundry room in the back and it seemed like nothing could stop her. I could hear Dean yelling and swearing and then—suddenly—silence.

Dean walked back into the kitchen, pale and shaken.

"I tried to shoot, but that stupid piece of shit gun jammed and nothing happened," he said. "She broke the window, grabbed the window ledge and started tearing the wall apart. She was coming for me, looking right in my eyes, and there was nothing I could do to stop her."

Once he realized the gun wouldn't fire, he said, he used it to beat her. "I used every ounce of muscle I had, hitting her as hard as I could, and it had zero effect, none!"

Just as he began to think we were both dead, she sat back on her hind legs, looked around, and stood up and lumbered away. The two- or three-year-old cubs followed behind her.

We were tempted to cancel our hike, as we were still in shock and afraid the grizzlies might have headed in the same direction. But it had taken me months to convince Dean to go with me and I found I couldn't make myself wait until the next time he might be in the mood. I added bear spray and a sharp knife to the contents of my pack, and we headed out as soon as we'd nailed sheets of plywood over the damage.

We drove our ATV across the valley and parked it at the end of the road, where we removed the seats and set them underneath. Oddly, bears love to chew them, so we put them under the tires.

We headed up the steep hillside on foot. We climbed for about an hour and a half, stopping occasionally to admire the views and take pictures of our camp from this new perspective. We could see our airstrip in the distance, and our machines at work, digging for gold in the cut.

We came to the rockface I had noticed when we first landed, and I threw down my heavy backpack. I began scouring the area for something, anything. It was a long shot, I knew that, but I'd felt indescribably compelled to come here. In what seemed like no time at all, I spotted a large Hill Bros. coffee can in a crevice, as if someone had just put it there for me to discover. I could barely make out the faded print through the rust. I shook it and could tell that it held something, but it was much too light to be gold. I somehow managed to pry off the lid using just my nails, and a musty, old-paper smell made me turn my head away—it was overpowering.

"Wow, that is strong," I said to Dean, who was standing beside me. "Do you think he put a treasure map in this can?"

I gently pulled a couple of pieces of paper out. Then, scared that I would drop or tear something important, I put them back in the can and stowed it carefully in my backpack. I'd look through it back at camp.

We combed the rest of the area, looking for more evidence of John's life here. We came across some wooden animal skin drying racks attached to the face of the rocks, but nothing else that seemed manmade.

After we'd explored for another few hours, looking in every crevice and under every stone, we ate our lunch and decided to head back to camp. I couldn't wait—all I could think about was the contents of my prized coffee can.

Dean dropped me off at the camp and I ran up the stairs to the kitchen, kicking off my boots. I swung my backpack off my shoulders and onto the table that overlooked the valley below. I could see the dust swirling behind Dean's ATV as he raced back to the sluice plant.

Pouring myself a cup of coffee, I sat down and pulled the lid off the can. This time I held it to my nose and breathed in deeply. It was an amazing smell, really—full of history, as if the past had come back to meet me. I carefully pulled out one piece of paper after another, shocked at how well it was all preserved. I realized that the heat from the sun had probably vacuum sealed the rusty can for more than sixty years, keeping the contents in pristine condition.

Some of the papers were letters in another language that I assumed was Norwegian. There was a book of unused Canadian stamps, a pocket-size notepad with random scribbling, and a metal eyeglass case with wire frames tucked inside. There were a few old photos, an address book, postcards, and a page from an unidentified restaurant menu.

I pulled out the original Declaration of Intention for John Matson's United States citizenship, sworn on the fifteenth day of January, 1896, and his original grant for placer mining, dated Dec 18, 1911.

It was such a strange mix of paperwork, and I wondered why he had kept and hidden these particular things. Near the bottom of the can I found a newspaper clipping that had obviously been read many times over. It was almost transparently thin and in a delicate state, so I was so careful as I unfolded it. The headline read, "*After 33 years, Klondike Kate weds sourdough.*"

My heart began to beat faster.

John Matson claims as bride the one he loved for 33 years - sail home tonight.

I couldn't believe what I was reading! Johnny Matson had married Klondike Kate? How had I never heard this before? The article went on to say that the pair's "nuptials" were held in North Vancouver, B.C, on June 17th, 1933.

I was astonished. It felt as if our new beginning on Matson Creek and my obsession with Kitty Rockwell had formed a protective circle I now lived within.

I finally shook the can to make sure it was empty, and heard something rattle at the bottom. I reached inside and pulled out a small black paper jewelry box. Its edges were worn and folded in; the sides had collapsed. John had wound a piece of string around it to hold it together.

Setting the brown string carefully on the table, I opened the box. The most beautiful chain lay upon a small piece of cotton. In the light from the kitchen lamp, I could see that it was decorated with tiny gold nuggets. All these years later, they still glittered brilliantly.

I heard Dean return and ran to the door, talking a mile a minute.

"What, no treasure map?" he said, teasing me.

"No, but look at this!"

After inspecting it closely, we realized it also had woolly mammoth ivory and a small coin with "California Gold 1849" inscribed on it.

I spent the next hour or so reading over each document again, finally going back to the article. I studied the picture of John and Kate at their wedding ceremony and, looking at his hands, I realized he was holding something. I jumped up and searched the kitchen drawers for a magnifying glass, the same one I had used earlier in the week to pull a deep sliver out of the palm of my hand.

Holding it to the newspaper, I could see the chain—he had worn it the day he wed Kate! And now I was holding it in my hands.

The crew started to arrive for dinner and I let them look carefully at my finds. They couldn't get over the fact that I had actually found something. Everyone knew how long people had searched the area for clues to the whereabouts of John's hidden gold. It made me feel as if John and I were somehow connected—as if he knew how attached I'd become to Kate and had put his real treasure in a place where I could find it.

A few days later I had to fly into town to drop off a gold shipment. I brought the Hills Bros. can to the Dawson City Museum and offered to donate some of the paperwork. After we talked for a while in her office, the curator asked if I would be interested in looking at the private files they had on Klondike Kate.

I jumped at the chance, of course, so she led me upstairs to a small room that held only a few filing cabinets and a wooden table with two chairs. She pulled a thick file from the cabinet.

Wishing me luck, she left me alone, closing the door behind her.

Among the many documents I examined were telegrams from Bend, Oregon, where Kate had lived at the time, to the Royal Canadian Mounted Police of Dawson City.

In one, she insisted that something must be terribly wrong with her husband, John. According to her, the gold deposit he normally wired to her account at that time of year had not been sent. She wrote that he would never fail to send her money.

In another telegram, after the RCMP had found his headless body on the trail to his remote cabin, Kate insisted that someone had murdered him.

The RCMP ruled that the death was natural, and that his head had been severed from his body when wolves pulled his corpse through the broken window of his cabin.

Kate wrote that John had a friend she felt was not a friend at all—she was sure he had killed her husband. If it wasn't murder, she asked, where was the gold he'd mined that season? Where were the furs that he trapped each year? And where was the gold chain that he never went anywhere without?

I gasped out loud.

I could not solve the mystery of John's missing gold and furs, or the manner of his death. But I did have the thing he held most precious, other than Kate. Tears flowed down my cheeks.

One of the men who worked with us had told me more about John Matson's story. After I learned that he was buried nearby, I visited his grave often, bringing bouquets of the wildflowers that grew in the valley. After finding the Hills Bros. can, I felt as if I was an emissary from Kate, that she somehow wanted me to remind him of her love for him.

His small headstone was engraved:

MATSON
In loving memory of John
1863–1946
Resting in the Yukon hills he loved

Sometimes I sang John a song, or told him what we were doing on his creek and how much gold we had found, or what part of the valley we were mining on and how it was going. After I knew they'd been married when he died, I told him that Kate had died peacefully in her sleep.

I wondered whether she had come to visit here. Though there was no record of a last trip to see her husband's gravesite, everything I knew about their relationship convinced me that she had and that she'd sat right here, perhaps picking similar bunches of wildflowers for him.

Later, when I was going through the roughest times with Dean, I would visit the gravesite and sit quietly, deep in my own thoughts, and talk to John and Kate.

It felt as if they listened to me, and I felt them around camp. My windshield wipers turned on by themselves when I drove the old pickup truck past John's grave. Once in the early morning as I cleaned the kitchen after breakfast, I was startled by what sounded like a large tow chain being thrown on the porch floor. I thought, *Who the hell was that*? Everyone had left for the mine. I opened the screen door and saw nothing. To this day, I believe it was John and Kate, trying to get my attention.

That day in the Dawson City Museum, I was consumed with figuring out what it all meant. Why was I the one to find John's valuables after so many people had failed?

I felt there was a reason for it all that I just couldn't understand—until much later, when I understood that Kate and John had somehow conspired to save my life.

CHAPTER FOURTEEN

Kate

I'd travelled across a whole country and much of another to make sure I would never be like my mother, so dependent on the man in her life that she'd send her own daughter away.

Yet here I was, walking away from my beautiful baby boy, heading back to a life that made no sense at all anymore.

I thought about those early years, when I'd tried to outsmart my mother, doing anything I could to shock the nuns until they sent me home. It was all I ever wanted then, to be home, with her. But she always found another convent to board me at, and when she finally took me all the way to Chile and left me there, I got the message—I was on my own. And if I was on my own, then I was going to enjoy life and travel the world.

Now I understand why my mother did what she did, but it doesn't make me feel better about finding myself in a similar position.

I never dreamt I'd love a man like I loved Alexander, but it isn't love that made me give up our child. If it was only love, I would go home to Dawson with this baby in an instant.

Alexander is my life now—I've invested all my money and my reputation in our future together. When he told me to get rid of the baby, I wanted to be the kind of woman who would walk away, but what was there to walk to? A life of shame and poverty? Starting all over with nothing again, but this time as a "fallen woman" with a "bastard"—what kind of life is that for a child? I wouldn't do that to my worst enemy, never mind a baby who stole my whole heart the moment I held him.

It had been too easy to let Alexander move in with me. I never doubted that we'd marry the moment we left Dawson City for civilization. He was crazy about me; he said he couldn't live without me.

In the Klondike, no one cared. It was all about the money there, all about the gold. If you were earning, you were respected, and if you weren't, you were pitied. Wealth was the only virtue.

In the North, I was Klondike Kate, and everything I did was just fine. Better than fine ... I was the closest thing to a celebrity north of Seattle, and I set the trends. If I lived out of wedlock with Alexander, that made it fine for any woman to live out of wedlock with her man in the Yukon.

When the dark-eyed bartender at the Palace Grand finally had enough nerve to talk to me and I found myself laughing at his jokes, it felt like I was being kind, being democratic. But he pulled me in. I thought I'd had big dreams, but Alexander dreamed in rainbows. From the first night we talked, he made me see myself on stages around the world, stages owned by the two of us. Using only his smooth cocoa voice and the liquid motions of his soft hands, he made me see the crowds and hear the cheers. The grand houses we'd live in and the trips we'd take were all incidental—together, he and I would be the biggest names in theatre. We would be remembered forever.

At first, Alexander was kind and a gentleman, even though he'd never been to school. Unlike many of the miners, I didn't feel I had to work to keep his hands off me. In fact, it was months before Alexander even tried to kiss me, and when he did, I'd been waiting for it so long it felt like I was dying of thirst and he'd offered me a cool, bottomless spring to drink from.

When he'd suggested that we were ready to buy our first theatre with my savings, I felt like it was the real start of our lives together. With the money we earned from the theatre, we would buy the next theatre, and with those earnings, the next. I'd be the star of the show until I didn't want to be anymore, a beloved chanteuse and dancer until I was ready to be a society lady.

I bought him the finest suits, hats and shoes. With my help, he could have passed for a European count. The poor, rough-edged bartender I'd met was no more, and when Alexander the theatre impresario suggested that we skip the formalities and "marry" by living together, I couldn't have been more delighted. All I wanted was to go to bed with him at night after a triumphant, ovation-inspiring show, and wake up to hear him planning the day's events. With the money we saved from his rent, he said, we could buy our next theatre even faster.

The months flew by, and when he started to cool toward me, I just worked harder. I dressed with even more care, showcasing my highlights, as they say. I laughed a bit louder at his jokes and was even more charming to the sourdoughs coming in with their nuggets, so the tip baskets overflowed at the end of each night.

It all seemed to be working until I told him I was going to have to take a bit of time off to have our baby.

I'd seen Alexander lose his temper occasionally, a quick explosion of rage over a piano player who missed too many chords or a barman who drank too much on the job, but I'd never imagined that rage would one day be pointed at me. I was his star, his belle, his beloved. I was his bank! But that night,

I was also his target. For those few minutes, that eternity, I thought he was going to kill me.

I expected the real Alexander to be back the next morning, to beg for forgiveness, to apologize and promise to never do such a thing again. But his face the next day was cold, and any warmth in his eyes was gone.

"You'll go south, Kitty. Have that child, and find someone to keep it. We'll lose thousands of dollars and push back our plans by years, but there is no other way. Train the best of the girls to take your place until you're back."

With that, he turned and walked out.

I was devastated that he didn't want our child, but I convinced myself that he would fall in love with his son (I knew it would be a boy, somehow) when I brought him back to Dawson City.

This was just a detour on our world tour.

It was only after I'd arrived in Spokane and seen the looks in peoples' eyes that I realized what I'd done.

My life was over if Alexander didn't marry me. If giving up little Alex was the price, then that's what I'd do. Otherwise, my son would grow up a bastard, and I'd be just an aging showgirl who'd foolishly given all her money to a man who didn't want her any more.

I went back to Dawson, but the light had gone out of me. I still loved Alexander, but I also feared him. I'd somehow become dependent on him despite earning almost all the money we'd invested.

I continued to dance and sing, but it was as if the miners could see my unhappiness through my smiles. And their money was drying up too—the easy gold was gone.

In the spring of 1902, Alexander told me he wanted to leave

Dawson to create a national theatre chain. By that time, I'd saved enough to buy something impressive in Seattle.

We decided that he'd go on to Seattle first and I would stay and run our interests in the Yukon. I didn't mind. I was saddened by the idea of leaving my friends, and this way we'd have money coming in even as we built the next theatre. Alexander had decided to call it the Crystal.

He hired people to write beautiful love letters to me during that long winter of 1902-03, since he still couldn't read or write in any of the five languages he spoke. In one of his letters, he said, "I can assure you, my dear, I shall ever think of you. I know you will me, and always hold you dear to me as at any time during our life."

I continued to work and send money south until 1904, when I finally insisted it was time to reunite with my husband.

It felt like time that we got an official blessing on our union, too.

I was excited to see our theatres. By then, Alexander had purchased three more venues. I was stunned when I arrived in Seattle and he told me that they still weren't bringing in enough money to keep themselves afloat—I'd have to find work. I went back to Spokane, where I knew people on the stage who could help. After living in Dawson City, the salaries I was offered seemed laughable, but they helped us keep the doors open. It was all temporary, Alexander said, and I believed him.

I'd been in Spokane only a few weeks when a friend came to me to show me a Seattle newspaper clipping.

"Alex Pantages, theatre magnate, weds young violinist, just seventeen years of age."

The slender, dark-eyed vaudeville performer looked like a child. Alexander was later quoted in the Seattle Times saying, "It wasn't until I met my wife Lois that I knew anything much about good women." He denied ever knowing Kate Rockwell.

There is no way to describe how shattered I was. After a few days of shock and tears, I called on a lawyer I knew, and he advised me to file a lawsuit. The irony was that, because we were seen as married by our community in Dawson, my money was Alexander's money. And since women weren't allowed to borrow money secured by property, all our theatres were solely owned by him. At the same time, because we weren't legally married, I had none of the legal protections of a married woman, as scarce as they were.

Nonetheless we sued for $25,000 in damages, which included some of the money I'd given him to invest and $1,000 for his breach of his promise to marry me.

As soon as the suit was filed, though, I felt even worse. I knew then that there was nothing that would ever heal the heartache and humiliation I felt. Had he ever loved me? Or was it just my earnings he'd loved? I had given up my child for him!

Of the next few years, I can only say that I wasn't myself. Though I was almost destitute, I went to collect my son, but it was too late—he didn't even know me and screamed when I took him from the arms of his foster mother. She begged me to leave him with her, and I knew she was right. I would only make his life worse.

Crying all day and walking the floors all night ruined my looks, and I was unable to find work. I admit that I reached for the bottle for comfort too often, and that left me hungover and bloated, looking twenty years older than I was.

Taking on a string of menial jobs, I eventually moved on to

Los Angeles, where I thought I might heal in the sun and find work, but LA was overrun with young and beautiful women who reminded me of Alexander's new wife.

One terrible night, I ran into him on the street. All of my old affection for him came rushing back when I saw him, and it felt as if he had to feel the same way about me. Had it all just been a horrible misunderstanding?

I told him how bad things had become and asked for his help. Even if he no longer loved me, surely he would remember my generosity.

He took six dollars out of his wallet and handed them to me with a look of disdain. Walking away, he said, "You don't look like much anymore, Kitty, but you could still earn a little on your back."

My friend Mary heard about my situation and wrote me a letter, sending it to my mother to forward on to me. One part spoke to me so clearly.

> *Please don't throw away your life because of one man. Don't make yourself something he will always be glad he was rid of. Make something of yourself, Kate, something he will wish he had kept!*

That paragraph saved my life. I realized how right Mary was—it was if I were busy proving to Alex that he'd been justified in betraying, robbing and abandoning me.

My lawyer finally advised me to settle with Alex out of court so that I could move on, telling me that I was unlikely to get much more and very likely to get nothing if I went to court. (Juries did not sympathize with unwed women in those days.)

It was not nearly enough, less than I'd spent on Alexander's clothes and hats. But my lawyer was right, as was Mary—I needed to move on.

I went back to Dawson City for a while, but everything I saw there reminded me of Alexander and my own foolishness. I had been a star, and a wealthy woman, and a mother—and I'd thrown it all away for a shyster. My mother had been right to try to protect me by sending me to convents.

I moved on to Fairbanks, Alaska, which was booming. I bought a hotel, but it burned to the ground during a fire that decimated most of the town in 1906. It was uninsured, so I was back to the stage and dance halls to make ends meet.

Meanwhile, Alexander rocketed to success. His name was well known across the country, and he owned twenty-six theatres by then.

I realized I couldn't go on recreating bits and pieces of my old life and call it "moving on." It was time to truly start over. I wasn't too old to have another adventure—I just needed a different direction.

Oregon! I became one of the first women in America to homestead alone, securing three hundred and twenty acres outside of Brothers, Oregon, in the high desert country.

To own the land outright, I had to make "improvements to the land and outbuildings," and oh, it was a lot of work. But one thing that people tend to forget is that dancing on the stage is demanding physical labour. I was ready, and I found that the work was tremendously healing. I killed Alexander Pantages over and over again with my sickle, and buried his body a thousand times with my hoe, alongside my own youthful stupidity. Eventually I was able to feel nothing except exasperation at my own foolishness. My friend Isobel and my mother had both warned me not to trust him, and I had been convinced they knew nothing about it. Ha!

In my new life, I lived in a one-room shack, but it was my shack. I'd never seen so much wide-open country in my life, nothing but sagebrush and sand as far as the eye can see. I fell in love with the desert sunsets and the huge blue sky, shimmering at the horizons.

In my dazzling ball gowns, dance costumes and slippers—because that's what I had—I dug and piled rocks and pulled sagebrush. There were many times I looked at the work ahead of me and almost gave up, but at the end of each day, I was both exhausted and cleansed. It was the happiest I'd been since the early months in Dawson City, and I realized I was content. My mother and son were taken care of, and I had a home I'd created with my own hands and sweat. I'd thought Alexander Pantages had taken everything I had, including my dignity. In the high desert, I found I had everything I needed.

In the fall of 1929, nine years after my mother had passed away, Alexander was charged with raping a seventeen-year-old actress seeking work at one of his theatres. By then he owned a controlling interest in twenty-eight theatres, in addition to the original twenty-six he owned outright. He was said to be worth more than ten million dollars. Unsurprisingly, he'd made a lot of enemies along the way.

To my astonishment, I was subpoenaed as a witness for the prosecution. By then I felt very little for Alexander one way or the other, but I burst into tears in court when I saw how old, thin and ill he looked.

Everything he'd done to me had clearly taken its toll on

him, too, and it hurt to see him laid so low. I didn't know if he was guilty of the rape—despite what he'd done later, he'd been a gentleman with me in those early days. Yet who knew what fame and fortune had made him?

It turned out that I never had to testify one way or the other. His enemies had their way, and the "Greek theatre magnate" was sentenced to fifty years in San Quentin prison. There he had a heart attack and was released after two years. It was said that he'd lost his fortune by the time he died, just five years after his release from prison.

Once again, "Klondike Kate" was back in the news, this time because of my appearance in his courtroom.

I would later learn that one of these disgusting articles was read by a hopelessly shy Norwegian miner, someone I'd met briefly many years before. How strange life is!

CHAPTER FIFTEEN

John

That Christmas Eve, I told myself I would marry the red-haired dancer no matter how long it took. I knew I had long queues of competitors, but I was a patient man.

I returned to watch Klondike Kate dance three times after that first night, but never had the chance to speak to her again. I was not a talkative man to begin with, English was difficult for me, and I found that love tied my tongue completely.

I lived a simple life, unaffected by the outside world. I worked hard on my claims for the next thirty years, collecting and selling gold and furs. Each summer I grew a flower garden, tending it in the hope that Kate would love it when I finally brought her home.

I occasionally went back to Dawson to buy supplies and deposit gold at the local bank, and on one of these trips, I was shocked to see a photo of my beloved on the front page of a newspaper.

"Belle of the Yukon to take the stand against former lover Alexander Pantages in rape trial," read the headline.

I read slowly, heartbroken as I learned of her troubles. I wanted to kill that man—how dare he desert her, and then bring her name into something like this?

The article ended by describing Kate's current life, alone

and nearly penniless on her homestead in the high Oregon desert.

My heart beat faster. I felt terrible for Kate, but I realized this was my time—it was our time. I could feel it as surely as I know the boundaries of my claim. I began quietly asking around town until I found one of Kate's old friends willing to pass on her mailing address.

I learned from her Dawson friends that Klondike Kate was now known as "Aunt Kate" to her Oregon neighbours. They knew of her previous life from the fascinating stories she told: mushing her dog sled through five feet of freshly fallen snow on the frozen Yukon River; invitations to reach into miners' "pokes" to pull out gifts of gold nuggets; watching the northern lights turn the night sky green and purple in circling waves of jewelled electricity. It sounded as if Kate still had a tremendous enthusiasm for life and adventure, and despite all of her troubles, lived without regret.

After the required seven years, she'd sold her homestead in Brothers and moved into town in Bend, Oregon. She had a quaint little house half a block away from the fire station, and she became a one-woman auxiliary, bringing hot coffee to the boys during fire calls and raising money to buy better equipment for them.

She loved raising money for neighbourhood causes, and discovered she was very good at it. Her celebrity as a "gold rush star" opened doors for her with the local business owners, and once they opened their doors, she used her charm to shake them down for generous contributions. She also spent many hours baking and making soup for hobos and the less fortunate.

She told me later how surprised she was to receive my telegraph.

My dearest Kate,

I have heard of your unfortunate circumstances and the loss of everything you invested in the Pantages empire. I met you one night in the Klondike many years ago. I can still see the wax in your hair as you twirled, and every detail of the dress you wore.
I have loved you, Kate, from that moment on.

In love only,
John Matson

I had no idea what to expect when I sent it. How would she remember someone she met for ten minutes thirty years before—someone so shy he couldn't speak to her at all? But she told me later that she did remember me, and my "kind and gentle eyes."

It didn't matter—something in the deepest part of my heart had always been sure that Kate and I would one day be together, and I knew now was that time. I hoped she would write or telegraph back, but if not, I would board up my cabin and head south if I had to.

To my great relief—because the truth was, I was not ready for the world outside of the Yukon—she telegraphed back. After that, we wrote often. There was never a time that I wasn't part way through a letter to her, and when I'd head to town to pick up the mail or someone kindly dropped it off to me, there were always multiple letters from her. I told her all about the changes in Dawson and described the wildlife and landscapes around my claim; she told me all about the people of Bend and her many charitable activities. With each word we exchanged, I loved her more.

Finally, in one of my letters, I asked her to marry me, promising to make her forget Alexander Pantages and to care for her and look after her as long as I lived. It took a lot of courage to ask, yet I felt it was fated.

I was the happiest man in the world when she wrote back and said, "John—of course! I would love to be your wife."

For just the third time since I'd arrived thirty-five years before, I left the Yukon.

We met in Vancouver, and I thought my legs would give out when she walked through the door. No longer young, she was even more beautiful in my eyes, her edges softened by her kindness. Her violet eyes sparkled like stars, and she still moved with the delicacy and grace of the dancer she was.

To the ceremony, I wore the finest clothes I'd owned in my life, purchased for the occasion—a black felt suit, polished leather shoes and a pearl grey fedora. I'd like to believe I looked handsome for her, and Kate's eyes seemed to say that I did.

She wore a blue crepe dress with cream coloured lace, tan shoes and a white hat. Together I hope we looked as we were—two people who knew they were meant for each other.

My hands trembled slightly as I placed on her hand the gold band, adorned with tiny nuggets I'd dug out of the Yukon creek beds myself. I knew that she would understand that they symbolized the best that I and the North could give her.

The ceremony started at six in the evening on July 14, 1933, and was a simple event with just a few guests. My best man was the secretary of the Vancouver Yukoner's Association, and an old friend of Kate's stood as witness for the bride. The Yukoner's Association presented Kate with a handsome purse, "Sourdough Union — Mush On," in block letters on the package.

When it was her turn to speak, Kate said, "I am marrying

the finest man in the world." I would argue that statement, but I readily admit that I am now the luckiest man in the world.

The following evening, we set out for home on the Canadian Pacific SS Princess Louise, a 331-foot steamship. It was a splendid small vessel that offered the class of service I was determined to provide to my new bride.

At dinner one night, the waiter in charge of our table mentioned how happy the two of us looked. I was sixty-nine and Kate was fifty-seven, yet I think that our love lit us both up from within.

Overcoming my natural shyness, I reached over and took her hand. "She means the world to me," I said after confirming that I was indeed the happiest of men. I somehow even managed to make Kate blush, which I didn't think was possible.

We arrived in Dawson City during the most beautiful time of the year, and after celebrating in town for a while, Kate accompanied me to my cabin. We made the most of the rest of that glorious summer, but when the weather showed signs of turning, I insisted she go back south. Winter was too hard for a lady, and we were fifty-five often impassable miles from the nearest doctor.

The truth is that we were also both used to living on our own by that time, and while we enjoyed each other's company very much, it wasn't too much of a hardship to go back to writing letters. I knew that she was the love of my life, and she knew that I would never let her suffer hardship again.

Each year afterward, we had a happy reunion in Dawson in the spring. Our conversations continued by letter, and so, while it was a delight to lay side-by-side, we felt as if we'd never been apart.

Every six months I sent a gold deposit south to help keep things in Oregon going smoothly for Kate, and once a year I'd travel down to stay for a while, bringing cured fur pelts from my trap line to keep her warm. I wanted to make up for every hardship she'd ever suffered.

After too many years apart, we were on life's great adventures together. Those were the sweetest years of our lives.

CHAPTER SIXTEEN

In my last year in the Yukon, my favourite job was driving into town for parts that were too heavy to fly in.

I drove a big four-wheel-drive truck and tried to break my own speed record each time. It usually took me around six hours; my fastest time beat that by thirty minutes.

We'd fixed up the road over the years and it was a lot easier to maneuver in a truck than in a giant excavator, but it was still a challenging trip. I took as many safety precautions as I could, carrying extra diesel, warm clothes, a blanket and pillow, food and lots of water. I learned how to change and fix flat tires because I'd often ruin more than one tire on that treacherous road. Because there were no ditches, melt and rain water ran like a river down the centre of the road, exposing huge jagged rocks that would then tear my tires to bits on the next trip out.

I usually left early in the morning and arrived back at camp after midnight. Occasionally I would stay the night in Dawson at Peggy's, but usually I was needed in camp the next day, so I had to get back on the road as soon as my pickups were done.

There were a few sections of the road that were decent, and it was there that I made up speed.

On what turned out to be my last trip out, I slid around a

dusty corner, the back end of the truck shooting out to my left as I pushed hard on the gas pedal.

Through my dust I saw a bull moose right in front of me, steam billowing from his massive body. I slammed on my brakes with both feet but was still sure I would hit him, probably killing us both. I managed to stop just fifteen or twenty feet away.

He stopped and looked back towards me for a few seconds before casually trotting away down the road.

I had my camera in the cab, so I followed him quite closely until he stopped, glancing back at me one more time. I put the truck into park and quietly opened my door so I could get a clear view, then started snapping photos.

It was still early morning and cold this high on the mountain. I was so close to him, and I was convinced these would be the best photos I had ever taken.

Apparently, this moose was camera-shy. He turned to face me, lowering his enormous head and antlers almost to the ground. Snorting loudly, he began to scrape his front foot on the muddy road.

He was going to charge me!

I didn't have time to put my truck in reverse, so I instinctively slammed my foot down on the gas pedal and the engine roared.

His antlers were much wider than the body of my truck, and as he picked up speed, I knew that I was going to be badly hurt at least. But just feet from the pickup, he changed direction slightly and ran up the hill to my left. I could have reached out and touched him as he went by.

He turned and bowed his head down once more, and I realized he was about to charge me again, this time aiming squarely at the driver's door.

I slammed the gear shift into drive, my truck sliding left and then right as I punched the gas, once again narrowly escaping the impact of his massive antlers.

Dean told me later that a moose of that size had enough power to shove a vehicle engine right into the front seat. I'll never know whether the moose's intent was to maim me, or if he was just scaring off the paparazzi the only way he knew how, but he certainly educated me about the dangers of getting too close to wild animals. In the North, even the ones that won't eat you might have a violent response to your unwanted company.

On my trip home that night, I saw a pair of eyes ahead, reflecting my headlights. Still shaken by the moose experience hours before, I wasn't about to rush up to whatever this was. As I got closer, I could see it was a lynx. They don't like people much, so we rarely saw them. I stopped the truck and turned off the engine, and he walked off the road and sat down directly beside me on the bank.

He was eye level with me and I rolled down my window very slowly. Quietly, I said hello. He just watched me, as curious about me as I was about him. The pretty tufts on his ears stuck straight up as he sat with me for a good fifteen minutes before padding away. He was beautiful, and his green eyes seemed to say that he understood what I was saying. I felt so happy after spending time with him.

It was almost as if he wanted to ease my fears after the moose encounter.

Up ahead was the worst section of the road. It had started raining after I left Dawson, which I knew would turn the road ahead into slick mud. The hills were steep and now it was dark.

I crossed a creek that was high from the rain and hit a muddy area I'd had problems with in the past. I approached slowly, making sure the tires on the driver's side were up on the bank, the dry ground giving me traction. But as soon as I started to make my way through, the back wheels of the truck slid into a huge, mud-filled crevice. I put it in reverse trying to back out, but I couldn't move. The crevice was so deep it swallowed half the truck, like slimy quicksand. The more I tried to move, the deeper I was mired in.

The driver's side was buried halfway up the door in slippery, clay-like mud. I had to grab the passenger seat and drag myself upwards to the passenger door, pushing it open with my feet.

I balanced on the running boards and jumped as far from the truck as I could, not wanting to fall into the mud hole myself.

Just as I steadied myself, I heard the distinctive howls of timber wolves, reminding me that this might not be the safest place to stand alone in complete darkness without any form of protection. I quickly emptied my overwrought bladder and climbed back up into the truck, slamming the door behind me to let the wolves know I'd heard them.

I had no way of communicating with anyone in camp, so I was stuck for the night. I bundled myself up with the extra clothing I'd brought and drew the blanket over me, trying to get comfortable and sleep.

I was startled awake a few hours later by the sound of animals sniffing around the truck outside. I could barely make out their grey and white colouring, but I counted four adult wolves. I sat perfectly still, thankful that I was safely inside with my groceries.

I knew they couldn't reach me in the cab, but it was still an eerie sight as they circled around me, over and over, until daylight.

Then they vanished silently back into the woods. I was grateful to see them leave, and waited as long as I could before cautiously jumping down from the truck to pee once again.

I sat outside for a while until I heard an engine winding its way down into the valley. I was extremely happy to see the red hood of the Mac truck coming to my rescue.

By the end of that trip, I felt like I was on top of the world. I felt empowered, like I could do anything. I had many hours to reflect that night, and I'd realized I was proud of myself and all that I had learned and accomplished over the years.

I had grown so much from the shy young woman who, because of leaving home so early, lacked many essential life and career skills. I'd credited Dean with making my dreams come true, but that night, I came to understand that this was something I'd accomplished on my own. Dean had brought me into the gold-mining life and I was very grateful to him for that. Since then, I'd often had to figure things out on my own, and I always had to push myself harder than I ever had before. I could run excavators, rock trucks, bulldozers and semis; I could chop firewood and change the oil in my truck. I could fix flat tires and shoot any type of gun. I was a bookkeeper and a great cook; I could even fly a plane in an emergency. I could write a cheque for over a million dollars and stake my own mining claims. For the first time, I realized that I admired the woman I'd become.

When I look back on that trip, it feels as if I was saying goodbye to the Yukon—and the Yukon came out to say goodbye to me.

A few days later Dean flew into town to drop off a gold shipment.

His pilot had already had a long day, exceeding the hours she was legally allowed to fly, but she decided to make one more flight. The small plane was also slightly overloaded, packed tightly with boxes. As they approached our airstrip, the low sun beamed through the clouds, blinding the pilot.

It was difficult to make out the airstrip below, but she tried to land anyway. As her wheels touched down, they could both see she'd overflown the runway, and the plane landed on the last half of the strip.

The pilot knew she was going to crash head on into the trees, so she panicked and tried to lift off again. Instead of avoiding disaster, she flew into the trees full throttle.

Dean was in the passenger seat as the Cessna 206 slammed from left to right, first one wing and then the other crashing into the trees. One wing was sheared completely off and the plane finally came to a stop upended, its nose buried in the ground.

Sure that the plane would burst into flames at any moment, they scrambled out. Somehow, they'd survived, miraculously, but Dean couldn't work for the rest of that summer because of searing migraine headaches, neck pain and confusion. He flew back to Dawson City right after the crash, but they didn't have the proper equipment to diagnose his injuries. The doctor examined him, palpating his neck area, and handed him some painkillers. He sent him back to camp, with a diagnosis of severe whiplash. We found out when we went south after the season ended that Dean's neck had hairline fractures in three different places.

I picked up as much slack as I could, trying to keep things going. It ended up being another bad year, with lots of equipment breakdowns and employee problems on top of Dean's injuries.

Worse than his pain was his rage. I couldn't seem to do anything right and we fought more than ever. It was unbearable for us both.

By the end of that season, I was sure that, if I continued mining with Dean, something bad would eventually happen. The early infatuation we'd felt for each other was gone, but I loved my husband and wanted to find a way to make our marriage work. I was committed to him and the life we had created.

I tried to convince him to see a counselor with me, but he refused.

Well, there was more than one way to solve a problem: that winter, we purchased a run-down commercial building in the centre of the town where we spent our winters.

CHAPTER SEVENTEEN

Ever the savvy entrepreneur, Dean had me train my replacement.

I'd convinced him that it wasn't a good idea for me to mine with him anymore, and that we should open a coffee shop in the town we lived in during the mining off-season. We renovated the building we'd purchased together over the winter. It was still a construction site when Dean left for the Yukon in the spring, but by the time he returned that fall, it was a booming business.

I worked eighteen-hour days, seven days a week, but my body didn't miss the pounding that heavy machine operators deal with every hour of their workday, that is for sure. That summer flew by.

Dean and I talked almost daily while he was away and I was so excited to have him home that fall. I was feeling good about myself—and I was so proud of our popular coffee shop. Life seemed really good. I told myself we were going to make it.

Because the coffee shop was doing so well, Dean decided we should open a marina and waterfront restaurant. He kept buying other businesses—a car wash, a grocery store, a storage business—and in the summer when he was away, I ran it all on my own.

Dean had always been ambitious, but nothing seemed to be enough for him now. Everything financed everything else, and it felt like a house of cards. Our monthly payments were outrageous, yet he spent money like his hero Donald Trump and bought himself a $120,000 Viper.

By the next fall I felt close to collapse and I told Dean we absolutely had to hire help. One day the following spring he called with a welcome surprise: he'd hired a new manager for the marina and waterfront restaurant. As soon as she was trained, it would be off my plate. Thank God!

It would have been nice to interview her myself, of course, but I liked Kimberly when we met. She reminded me of a younger me—she learned fast and worked hard. She even looked like a younger me, pretty and blond with a bright smile, always in motion. I was impressed by her enthusiasm, and her husband seemed like a great guy—I looked forward to the four of us being good friends.

One day a few months later, Dean called from the mine and asked me to give Kimberly a week off before the busy summer season started. It was a good idea—I knew we'd both be flat out once tourist season hit. I was touched that he was thinking in terms of potential burnout—it seemed he'd actually paid attention when I talked about the importance of rest and recovery to alleviate my chronic pain.

Minutes after he called, she came into my office.

"Dean said he talked to you about me taking a week off?"

Wow, news travels fast.

"Yes, of course! When do you want to go? Do you have any fun plans?"

"Um, right now! I'm just going to stay with a girlfriend for a week—drink wine, catch up, relax."

There was something awkward going on between us, but I couldn't figure out what it was. It was as if she couldn't get out of my office fast enough. Kimberly was super uncomfortable with me all of a sudden. It made me wonder: why hadn't she talked to me about taking time off in the first place, rather than going to Dean?

I saw the hostile glare of Dean's Honduran security guard once again, and felt the same cold fear, deep in my spine. Something wasn't right.

I kept telling myself I was wrong, but by the next day, I couldn't bear not knowing. I called our usual pilot in Dawson.

"Hey Cliff ... I just wanted to make sure yesterday's flight went okay."

"Yep, we got your new cook in to camp no problem."

There was no new cook.

When Dean finally returned my calls a few days later, he yelled at me for trying to ruin Kimberly's life (I'd called her husband to see if he knew anything). After a few minutes of me crying and him yelling, he told me it was over between us. Kimberly was "the one."

I fell into the so-called stages of grief, shattered. It wasn't until it was over that I really understood how much faith I'd had in Dean—how naive and trusting my love for him was. Even after everything that had happened between us, I still believed that we were partners forever.

Somehow, I even believed he'd be fair with me when we separated. There was a small house on the storage business property, so I moved out of our 11,000-square-foot waterfront home into the beat-up 1960's tear-down. We agreed that I'd keep and run the coffee shop and storage business; he'd take the rest.

Everything was heavily financed at interest rates that made it impossible for the businesses to cover their costs and the payments, but Dean said he'd manage the interest with income from the real money-maker, the mine.

He did not. It all went into foreclosure—everything. I was left homeless and without an income; the stress and depression caused a chronic pain flare-up worse than anything I'd experienced before, and made it impossible to look for a new job.

Repeating a strategy I'd once admired, Dean bought everything back at auction—for a fraction of what was owed.

I'd managed to put a bit of money aside during our marriage, enough to keep me afloat until I found work, but it all eventually went to lawyers. I won every court case, but it made no difference. Despite living like a king and pulling gold out of the ground every year, Dean insisted he was penniless. The courts were never able to find anything in his name to seize.

At the end of a decade of backbreaking work, side by side, he had a mansion on a lake, a mine and a newer-model blonde wife. I had nothing but my grief and pain.

I don't think I would have made it if it weren't for Kate. If you've been heartbroken in that particular way, you know how it destroys your faith in life and yourself. The betrayal is searing, like being burned alive from the inside.

I thought often of Kate somehow surviving what Alexander Pantages had done to her. Each time my situation seemed unbearable, when I didn't think I could go on, I'd return to the letter her friend Mary sent to her.

> *Please don't throw away your life because of one man. Don't make yourself something he will always be glad he was rid of. Make something of yourself, Kate, something he will wish he had kept!*

It's one thing to intend to "make something of yourself" and another thing to make that happen, though. I was focused almost entirely on our divorce case and it was like living in a toxic dump.

One day, I was over at a friend's helping him pack up after his own divorce. In his garage was a Harley Davidson motorcycle, covered with dust and dirt, that he'd bought for his wife early in their marriage. She'd never ridden it—it was fifteen years old but only had seventeen kilometres on it, the distance from the dealership to their house.

I'd never ridden a motorcycle, never even thought of riding a motorcycle, but I felt an instant kinship with that beautiful machine. I thought about Kate in the high desert, the dry winds blowing her hair back as she worked the hard ground.

I saw myself on the highway, travelling to the many places I'd yet to see in the Pacific Northwest. I felt a deep knowing, down in my bones—this would be my homestead, my new beginning.

I had no money, but I sold all my gold nugget jewelry and the ruby and diamond monstrosity that Dean had bribed me with in Honduras. It was just enough for the bike and motorcycle classes.

I put twenty-two thousand kilometers on it over the next

two years, riding alone up and down the coast.

Each time I felt the wind lift the hair that escaped my helmet, I'd feel a bit of my life with Dean blowing away behind me. I felt lighter, freer and younger as the miles passed by.

As I travelled, I got to know myself again, or—perhaps—for the first time.

When Kate's life was stolen from her, she created a new one. Why not me?

Fortunately, I didn't have to wait until my late fifties to find my own version of John Matson, a kind and gentle man who wanted my happiness as much as his own.

EPILOGUE

In the end, Kate taught me that the most powerful words in the English language are, "I forgive you."

After Dean switched wives and made it clear that he'd stopped feeling anything like love for me some time before, there were times when I believed there was no way to go on. It wasn't just that he was proving, over and over, in increasingly cruel ways, that he did not care about me—it was that I had made him the centre of my life. When he left, I realized I'd given him the power to tell me who I was.

How could I rebuild my life when I couldn't trust myself ? And how could I trust myself when I was so completely wrong about what he and I meant to each other?

I kept going back to Mary's letter to Kate, the one that lifted her out of despair. It reminded me that it was up to me to heal myself—but it didn't tell me how.

One day, filled with bitterness and hurt, I thought about what I'd read about Kate when she was called to testify against Alexander Pantages. She reported afterward that she *cried* to see him "brought so low."

It took a while, but it finally sunk in. She was moved by his hardship because she had forgiven him. Not because he deserved her forgiveness, and certainly not because he'd done anything to earn it. Kate forgave him, I'm convinced, because she learned that it was the only way to free herself.

It feels so important to hang on to betrayal. It's as if we can't move on until the person who harmed us says, "I see you. I see how much you've suffered and that you didn't deserve it."

Of course, that is impossible. If they were the kind of person who could truly see us, they wouldn't be the kind of person who could betray us.

At the end of our marriage, Dean had the mine, the mansion, the money—all the material things. Yet he was still the man who could have everything and yet feel hungry for more. And I'm guessing that Kimberly is now experiencing the same kind of hopeless burnout I did while trying to fill that void.

I will always miss the Yukon, and I treasure the memories I have of that time. In court, over and over, I tried to get Dean to acknowledge that what we'd done there together was worth something to him—and I had to learn to live without that acknowledgement.

It was only when I thought about Kate crying in court that I realized what she and I had, that could never be taken away from us: We had learned that we were more than enough on our own, and that we knew how to live a happy life.

I've always known more than I thought I did about happiness, but witnessing the havoc Dean created in our lives was the most powerful lesson of all. In the end, the most important thing he taught me was that nothing matters without kindness and true partnership. As painful and unjust as the divorce was, he freed me to go out and find the kind of love he had promised and wasn't capable of providing. And I did.

This book began when friends told me, over and over, that I must write about my time in the Yukon. I imagined it all as a movie: part *Moulin Rouge*, part *Into the Wild*, part *Legally Blonde.*

It wasn't until I started writing that I realized the true power that writing holds.

First, we tell our stories. Then, with twenty-twenty hindsight, we come to understand them. And when we do, we turn our sorrows into strength. With that new strength, we create the lives we dream of.

By the time John Matson reached out to Kate, she'd learned how to be happy. The man she chose to share her life with was kind, steady and devoted. Her happiness was his happiness.

Kate inspired me in so many ways as we built our lives in the North. In the final chapter, though, it was her life after the Yukon that saved me—she taught me how to begin again, and thrive, and love.

In this, we are just two links in an endless chain of women who have been betrayed and gone on survive, thrive and find greater happiness. History has forgotten so many, but more and more, we're seeing women's truth written into history, with the power to free us all.

Last month, my love and I took delivery of a new rescue animal: a miniature donkey. He joined our small menagerie of rescued strays, furry friends we've committed to love and care for, for the rest of their lives. We love those animals and each other the way we want to be loved—the way everyone deserves to be loved—fiercely, and with complete acceptance.

Because—as Kate proved—the only love worth having is the kind that gives us room to grow and makes us free.

ACKNOWLEDGMENTS

I am so grateful to my parents, Joan and Walter, for gifting me an open mind with which to approach this thing called life, and for all of their support over the years.

To my son, Christopher—thank you for always believing in me. I love you to the moon and back!

To my fiancé, Norbert—without your love and patience, I would not exist.

To my editor, Lori Bamber, I would like to extend my profound gratitude.

And finally, to Anna Mullens, for igniting the spark. I admire your work and will always be grateful we met.

I would also like to acknowledge my past. Without it, there wouldn't be a story.

SELECT REFERENCES

Although the books I've enjoyed reading about the Klondike over the years are too numerous to include here, I'm especially grateful to the authors of the following titles, those I relied on most when learning about Kate's life.

Good Time Girls: Of the Alaska/Yukon Gold Rush
Lael Morgan, 1998, Epicenter Press

Women of the Klondike
Frances Backhouse, 1995, Whitecap Books

Klondike Women: True Tales of the 1897–1898 Gold Rush
Melanie J. Mayer, 1989, Swallow Press

Klondike Kate: The Life and Legend of Kitty Rockwell, The Queen of the Yukon
Ellis Lucia, 1962, Hastings House Publishers

ABOUT THE AUTHOR

Brandee Radford's parents moved often throughout her childhood, eventually settling in the small town of Lillooet in British Columbia, dubbed "Mile 0" of the historic Gold Rush Trail.

She left home in her mid-teens, searching for love, adventure and acceptance. In the wilds of the Canadian North, she finally found the place that felt like home, and she mined for gold there for more than ten years.

In *The Chain*, she follows in the footsteps of her father, who loved to write, capturing her electrifying Canadian wilderness life alongside that of her role model, Klondike Kate Rockwell. (Researched and re-imagined, often in Brandee's hardest hours.)

She now lives on the shores of the South Thompson River in Kamloops, BC, with her fiancé. Together they care for a small herd of rescue animals on their hobby farm. (But not bears.)

Find her at Gold Nugget Woman on Facebook and Instagram.